Candle Making Business 102

DRIVE GROWTH THROUGH SOCIAL MEDIA MARKETING AND IN-PERSON SELLING. LEVERAGE TIKTOK, INSTAGRAM, PINTEREST, ETSY, SEO, EMAIL MARKETING AND FARMERS MARKETS TO YOUR ADVANTAGE.

Grace Holmes

ABOUT THE AUTHOR

Grace is half-Greek, half-English, and is passionate about escaping the nine-to-five norm and helping you do it, too.

Grace is an authority on candles because she understands the business side of candle making after studying Business and Economics in-depth for four years. After making candles as a hobby, she decided to combine her two passions, business and candle making, to start a new business.

She can confidently say that she knows what she is talking about because she has been working in Brand Strategy and Marketing for years and understands how to make your brand stand out from competition. This, coupled with growing and running an Instagram business for six years, gave her a wide knowledge into digital marketing.

Her main goal is helping you to achieve candle making business success. She believes that this matters deeply because starting a business can be so overwhelming, and it's very hard to know where to start and how to succeed. Many people sell candles these days, so it's difficult to stand out from the competition. However, by making guided business choices, you can create an extremely lucrative business.

Grace believes that she is the right person to be writing this book because she is passionate about turning what you love into something that can make you money. It is extremely hard to start a business on your own without guidance and learning from experts. She believes this is how you have faster and more sustainable business success.

According to Grace, "I'm writing this book because I am passionate about helping others make their candle making business a success, as the majority of small candle making companies miss out on so many sales due to focusing solely on the technical side of candle making, and I do not want you to be one of them."

A FREE GIFT TO OUR READERS!

A free copy of **11 Easy Tricks to Master your Candle Launch and Triple your Sales within the First Month!**

Visit this link to get your copy now:
www.graceholmesbook.com

CONTENTS

INTRODUCTION

A long time ago, I found myself stuck in the same repetitive cycle. Regardless of how cheery Dolly Parton sounds when she sings it, the 9-5 sucks. I'd spent four years of my life studying Business Economics just to become a desk jockey. I figured I needed something to wake me up inside and save me from corporate life. To my surprise, I found that in candle-making. I'll be honest, I kind of scoffed at the idea at first, but I quickly realized I loved it.

As time went on, I grew more invested in making candles than I did my actual job. So, I made a bold move. I chose to combine my love of candles with my knowledge and passion for business and create something of my own. The result? Well, here I am now, typing the introduction to you in my second book on how to run a thriving candle business. Initially, I was just like you are at this very moment. I needed guidance and insight. I kept getting told what I was doing was foolish and just not going to work. Sound familiar? If I had listened to all the people who doubted me, I wouldn't have fully embraced my role as an entrepreneur in a niche like candle-making. That's an alternative reality I'm not interested in even considering!

If you've ever been told there's no way of making a passion a career, then you're being lied to! You bought this book which means on some level you know they're wrong and now it's time to seize every opportunity right in front of you to claim your spot in this fabulous industry.

This book is for all the candle makers interested in getting into the business of making and selling their beautiful products. It's also for those who've been doing this for a while and finding little to no success. You're faced with a choice of either throwing in the towel or implementing changes to rejuvenate your business and keep that flame alive. I'm glad you're reading this book, it means you're not entirely ready to give up, and that's a start!

No matter what issues you're currently facing on your journey to success, there are solutions. We're going to get to the bottom of why things aren't working and how to turn it all around. Then, I'll show you how to revive your business before exploring all the ways you can market your brand and products. Get ready; this is going to be one heck of a ride from start to finish. You're about to learn all about the wonderful world of social media marketing. You're going to learn how to thrive online, utilize influencers, embrace wholesale, start email newsletters and so much more! You'll never have to ask yourself, 'where do I start with marketing' ever again.

My name is Grace Holmes and I am now on a mission to liberate you to follow your own candle making dreams! I've experienced the intense workload of starting a new business and I know just how overwhelming it all can be when you're just getting started. It's even worse because everyone, and their mother, is making a candle, it seems at the moment. It's harder to stand out now than it was when I started, but that doesn't mean it's impossible.

There are so many ways to crack into untapped markets, audiences and spaces to find an audience. The internet is a big place and the world is even bigger. I'm incredibly passionate about turning passion into profit without the sacrifice of integrity or enjoyment. My goal with this book is to provide you with the tools you need to show the world what your brand is all about. It's time to take this dream and turn it into a reality far bigger than you ever even imagined! I'm tired of the missed opportunities I constantly encounter when talking to other creatives in this niche. It's time to claim every avenue of business and maximize your capabilities as a candle business owner. Before we get there, we have to assess where you currently stand and how we can improve on the foundational aspects of your business. So, let's get you moving on this journey towards complete and utter success!

Chapter 1: Is Your Business Optimized and Ready to Seize the Internet?

The number one rule of owning and operating a candle business should always be passion. However, passion sadly only gets you so far. To really make the most of this incredible skill you've acquired and honed over the years, you need a basic understanding of how business works, and more importantly, how to make your business work efficiently.

In this chapter, we're going to explore the economics of business. I want you to strip your new or current business down and start from the foundation before building up to where you can look to the future!

Let's start, shall we?

Turning a Profit

Who doesn't love to see their business making far more money than it's losing? I really hope the answer is *everyone*!

A profit occurs when you minus **costs** from your **revenue**, and if the revenue is greater than the cost you will make a surplus (profit). So if the revenue is low, but the costs are high, then you could be looking at a deficit, and your business makes a loss.

Before you lock the doors and pack up shop, take a moment to stop and understand what contributes to a thriving revenue and how to optimize your costs.

How To Decrease Your Candle Business Costs

There are so many ways you can go about decreasing your costs to produce candles that retain their quality while maximizing the profit margins. So let's explore some of those options that can make your business just a bit, or hopefully a lot, more profitable.

Bulk Buying

There is no denying that suppliers love bulk buyers and are willing to reduce rates once you have hit a large order quantity to secure orders. Using the logic of economies of scale, sometimes you can see drops of nearly 20% in the final price tag purely because you've doubled your order.

It can be really easy to get thrown off by the hefty price tag of the initial order, but if you take the time to look at the cost per unit, you'll see the savings you're achieving. The less you're paying for essential items like; wicks, wax, jars, fragrance oils, dyes, and more, the better your profit margins.

Stamps & Stickers

I understand your desire to stand out and make your brand super personal but remember that this can set you back considerably in some cases. The more detail that goes into packaging and 'thank you' notes is time taken away from running your business, all while driving the cost per item up considerably.

Remember, you can't set ridiculous prices for your products; otherwise, demand will decrease, and so will your revenue. On the other hand, if your boxes and 'thank you' cards cost a fair chunk of change, you're harming your bottom line. Saying this, it is important to take time to create a brand story, if your packaging is boring it is hard to stand out. An alternative way to spice up your packaging are stamps and stickers, they are great to show some love to your customers at a lower cost.

Cost-Effective Delivery Options

The post office can be a bit of a bummer when it comes to the cost of deliveries. However, if you're handling deliveries yourself, then maybe it's best to do some research and find the cheapest shipping options;

For starters, make sure you're charging money for delivery or factoring delivery costs into your price point. My favorite shipping option is to use 'Pirate Ship' to get the cheapest pricing. Additionally, USPS offers free pick-ups, and you're able to print your own labels, which is just an additional financial score! If you want more information about shipping, there is a whole section dedicated to the subject in my first book 'Candle Making Business 101'.

Pro Tip:

> Get a thermal printer, they don't use any ink and you can print out your shipping labels and other decorative labels extremely cheaply, all you need to buy are the stickers (loads of options on Amazon).

How To Increase Your Candle Business Revenue

There are so many ways you can go about decreasing your costs to produce candles that retain their quality while maximizing the profit margins. So let's explore some of those options that can make your business just a bit, or hopefully a lot, more profitable.

White Labeling

White labeling can become a great source of additional revenue. The process is relatively simple, you make a standard candle and someone else buys it off you and brands it themselves. You can sell your brand of candles with funky designs, scents, etc., while also fulfilling custom orders. Custom orders could be for other stores, hotels, restaurants, and various other options where their branding is on the candle.

Don't Be Afraid of Outsourcing

If you think I expect you to be an artist with a camera like you are with candle making, for example, then you're wrong. Outsourcing can be great as they come with experience in product photography/videography. They can bring ideas to the table and create content that is of the highest quality.

If you're posting terrible content, you're going to lose the interest of your potential customers. In no way, shape, or form is that what you're aiming to do, so hire professionals if your budget allows it. My favorite platform for this is Fiverr.

The True Value of Your Time

If you're a control freak, I have some bad news for you. You need to start considering additional help.

There is no shame in hiring someone to help you improve your business presence online (and even offline). While initially, this will cut into your profits, the long-term benefits can be immense for growth. This makes the investment of someone to lighten your workload almost essential. This doesn't mean a full time member of staff, it could be a social media manager if you would rather focus on other aspects of your business. If you want to be the one doing social media marketing, then hire someone who can take over some of your other responsibilities such as candle making, packaging, writing copy or taking your photos.

Your time matters, and whatever you choose to focus it on, it needs more than just your limited 'free time.'

You can’t burn the candle at both ends… literally! Just remember time vs. money, is this task more effort than it's worth? If so, outsource.

Social Media Is Your Ally, Not Your Enemy!

Candles are an aesthetic product before anything else. That little flicker of ember, the shapes, attractive designs you’re known for, it’s all so social media ready. Nobody is asking for you to be the top ‘Candle Influencer.’ Still, if you think social media doesn’t matter, you’d be sorely mistaken.

Platforms like Pinterest and Instagram are craving some of the aesthetic shots of your beautiful creations. While not every engaged viewer will buy a candle, a percentage of them will. So you’d be able to wedge yourself into an untapped market for your business and get to have fun candle photoshoots, win-win if you ask me. I will speak in detail about social media in the next chapters, so don’t worry, all the details you need to smash it are coming.

A Killer Website and Flawless SEO (Search Engine Optimization)

Not having a website or Etsy shop in this day and age is really uncommon, so I hope you’re not in the minority of businesses going without a trusted online presence. Sell your candles directly to your customers online with a sleek website. Make sure your website’s filled with SEO-perfected listings and content to become a high-ranking member of the candle niche Google society. Again, chapter 3 is completely dedicated to SEO so don’t worry if you don’t know anything about it yet!

A Product List Filled With Options

If you've got the capital to invest in your brand further, INVEST in new product options to widen your product range. Look at competitors, find ideas to reinvent the wheel, and put your own unique spin on candle designs, scents, shapes, and sizes, to cater to more people who might be looking for candles that are more than just the standard candles they see or smell.

Rebrand

Rebranding is a big decision, but sometimes it becomes the necessary 'nuclear option.' If your business is struggling to the point where your methods of improving sales aren't landing, you need to dig deeper. You need to ask yourself the following questions;

1. Is my product unique?
2. Is my store professional?
3. If I were a customer, would I buy from my store?
4. Is my brand message clear and consistent?
5. Do I actually have an identifiable message?
6. Does my brand have a clear identity or none at all?

If you answered no to any of these questions, you NEED to rebrand. These questions may not all carry the same weight, but they all are essential regardless as they determine if consumers care about your product or brand.

In order to move forward, you need to go back to the start and reevaluate your business. As you review how your business operates, what image it promotes, and all the finer details that are either weighing you down or propping you up.

Optimize your business to the fullest possible extent and create/recreate a strong, clear, engaging, and forward-thinking brand. The past is great for memory's sake, but it's lousy for growth if you don't learn from mistakes and successes.

Pro Tip:

> Start at the basics first, reevaluate your customer profile and make every decision based on your ideal customer and what *they* want. Once you've managed to achieve everything you set out to achieve, you can start moving on to promoting a brand you're proud of and, more importantly, believe in.

Key Takeaway

Fair warning, ignoring these first few pivotal steps and jumping right into social media marketing is a recipe for disaster. If you're marketing a brand that isn't able to spark interest and joy in the real world, it will flounder on the internet. You'll spend mountains of money and have a disappointing ROI (return on investment) that will not only demotivate you to improve but will also sink your business faster than the Titanic.

If you've checked all the boxes and are ready to promote your fantastic brand, then let's get moving! It's time to start diving into the wild world of social media marketing.

Chapter 2: The Power of Product Photography

A picture is worth 1000 words

For any business that wants their products to thrive, you need to have killer photos that show off your products in the best possible way. You've made some great candles, spent so much time and effort on your brand; why would you douse the flames when you've gained all this momentum?

There is no way to progress to the next level without the right tools, and while having an optimized business is the most crucial aspect of getting to that next level, the thing that can make or break your progress is lack of quality with your product images.

In this chapter, we're going to be exploring product photography. What is it? Why is it important? What are the benefits? How to do it right?

What is Product Photography?

Product photography is the process of taking photos of a product with the intention of using it to help sell said product.

The whole concept of product photography is to showcase what you and your business offer to bridge the divide between consumers and the product, which is usually evident in an online transaction. Considering you can't see the product physically, you need to make educated decisions based on the information you're given, which includes a series of product images. Additionally, the photographed products are usually repurposed for online social media use, marketing campaigns, emails, and even print.

While there are two variations of product photography, standard, and eCommerce product photography, they both serve a near-identical purpose and overlap more often than not.

Why is Product Photography Important?

Sales are all about convincing customers that your product or service is worth purchasing. Now, I don't think I need to tell you this, but there are a lot of candles out there available to buy right now. I believe your candles are the bomb, but I'm biased. I'm here to hype you up and to help you sell *more* candles. Potential customers often need an extra push to get them to the point of sale… especially when they probably don't *need* more candles.

While there are so many reasons why product photography matters, here are the main reasons why it's a vital step in your journey to growing your business.

Introduction To Your Brand

First impressions matter and when a customer sees your business or product for the first time, they make an immediate value judgment based on the aesthetic values of your products. As a result, you need to ensure your product images are high quality, easy to understand both at a glance and with deeper inspection and represent your candles as accurately as possible. A candle next to a diamond is going to make for a confusing and disappointing purchase. Covering up your mistake and changing Marilyn's quote to 'candles are a girl's best friend', won't save you. Your lack of clarity will make your aesthetic choices a hard lesson to endure.

Tells The Story of Your Brand

You need to consistently represent your brand, seeing as product images will be on the frontlines of this, good photography is vital. A clear consistent brand message through language and photography is key. You need to ensure your brand is properly represented and is getting positive feedback. If not, listen to your customers' complaints and don't ignore them.

Converts Connection into a Sale

Product images pique a consumer's interest. Hopefully, a relationship between the consumer and your company is born in the process. Furthermore, with product photos usually acting as the first taste of the product, you want that customer to develop a bond where they become almost obsessed with having the product you're selling. Connection is like engagement, and how you build on the connection is the difference between a sale and a customer walking away.

Fills The Void of the In-person Shopping Experience

As I've mentioned already, product photos act as the bridge between online shopping and in-person shopping. Product photos are as close as a customer can get to seeing the product up close if they haven't already. Of course, that's a lot of pressure to put on a photo, but it's this way for a reason. You need to be able to confidently say you've put your best foot forward and released product photos that showcase your product in the best possible way allowing consumers to really get a feel for what they might purchase. Some buyers base their *entire* purchase on the product photos. Good product photography can increase your conversion rate by 30% (Bhatoa, 2021). You have far more to lose by not taking your product photos seriously.

Enhances Your Marketing Copy and Product Descriptions

Words matter, but in this case, not as much as pictures. The truth is, a lot of people aren't a fan of reading unless they really have to. Are you reading this for fun? My point exactly.

I'm not saying recreational readers don't exist. But even recreational readers aren't going to devour your product descriptions. Why? Because product descriptions are inherently boring as all hell. There's only so much you can do to fix that, but the main point is that a picture can seal the deal. The product copy will just describe an item in technical details. You're not trying to win an award for your product descriptions so take several steps back. Instead, treat the pictures as striking and beautiful representations of what the text explains in semi/non-entertaining sentences. Words can only achieve so much, and they're simply not enough to seal the deal when it comes to sales.

Additionally, you're getting your money's worth from the product photos you produced. Content should always be utilized more than once. Work to make your content capable of being enjoyed across multiple platforms like TikTok, Instagram and Pinterest.

Makes a Product More Attractive, More Alluring

When it comes to your product photography, you need to ensure you're getting the best quality to make selling your product more accessible. Focusing on high-resolution colors, multiple angles, close-ups, and anything that makes the product stand out as something that demands attention.

There's a two-step approach to making your product more attractive. The first step is to show off the product in a straightforward manner to eliminate all potential mystery about what the product is and what it looks like. Secondly, it's putting it in settings to sell the lifestyle associated with that product. Nothing gets the taste buds tingling, or in this case, the matches trembling, like a product photo that sells your customer a lifestyle that perfectly matches theirs.

Imagine a picture of a happy family enjoying dinner with your candles in the center of the table, lighting up their smiles and a home cooked meal. The image is warm and inviting, with the candles being the main focal point. Now the candles in no way come with a family, a lovely house, a family pet, or anything like that, but one can dream. People can assume that candles are part of the checklist to get the whole scene. So remember who your target audience is and create photos which you think they may desire.

Improves Marketing Strategy Effectiveness

The power of fantastic imagery can extend far beyond your e-commerce store. Using the images you create for your online store across various media platforms allows you to reach new audiences while remaining consistent and on-brand. Good product photography is 40% more likely to be shared from your social media accounts (Bhatoa, 2021). Gaining likes, and shares, and tags will organically grow your audience online, which is what you want. You want to get a response from people and convert them into customers. If you're consistent in your output in terms of quality, creativity, clarity, and value, then the sales will follow.

Increased Authority

The more you give your customers, the more they build trust with your brand. It's a delicate balance as you don't want to overload them with thousands of images for your entire catalog. However, the more information you provide, the more they will trust what you're selling and will be confident in their purchase.

Additionally, with more resources available to understand the products you have to offer, you increase your authority as a retailer. People will look at your brand as one that knows what they're doing, what they're selling, and this can be the edge you need over your competitors.

Professional, well shot, consistent product photos communicate to consumers that your business is legitimate, diverse, innovative, and has value and quality. Every good photo builds trust with the consumer helping to gain their sale.

Ask yourself that all-important question; 'have I bought a product online because of a great product photo?' I know I have. I won't get into those purchases because I don't need to relive the ghosts of purchase past - let's just say they were questionable. However, you want it to be a situation where, out of all the options, you're giving people the most clear-cut view of what's on offer and who you are.

10 Tips for Better Product Photography

You now know why photography matters, but now it's time to learn more about how to take your product photography to the next level. So here are ten tips for better product photography that I live by.

1.Show Off Options

If you have a candle that comes in different colors and styles but fits under one product, you need to show off all the available options. Imagine you found out later that your favorite purchase came in a better color, size, or design? I don't know about you, but I'd be pretty disappointed in the company that sold it to me for not disclosing all the available options. Don't just take one photo of the base option or most popular variation, and call it a day. When you ignore the options, you lose people who might have actually purchased the product had they known there was something more suited to their tastes.

2. Embrace Rule of Thirds

If you don't know what the rule of thirds is, then it's time to learn. The concept of the rule of thirds is a guide to creating an image where viewers are drawn to the picture's subject. In this case, they're drawn to your candle. The rule of thirds composition calls for an image to be divided into thirds both horizontally and vertically. This subject of the image is then placed on the intersection of the dividing lines or along one of the lines themselves to draw attention to them instead of the surroundings that act as a transition. Thus, the rule of thirds creates a fuller picture for consumers to see not only the product but the image overall, enhancing their appreciation of the product, albeit subconsciously.

3. Utilize Props

Don't go crazy. You're taking photos of your candles, not crafting the next music video for Katy Perry. Instead, use some basic props to create a complete image that showcases the product's practical use. For example, a candle is great for romantic dates. So you can use some people on a date with a blanket, or at a table, some rose petals, etc. Always use props that fit the image's narrative and serve the product in showcasing its use.

4. Make Sure You Have Proper Lighting

The irony considering candles primary use, but lighting can't be understated. Nobody cares if your candle can light up a hallway, so when I keep saying show off a product's practical use, I don't mean like this. You need images that showcase the products and leave no room for squinting to see what the candle says or what the design looks like. If a moment's thought has to be inserted into viewing a product image, you've likely lost them.

5. Edit Your Images Just The Right Amount

Don't go at your product photos like you would a selfie on Instagram. You're selling these products, and if you make it look different than it really is, well, you're in for some negative feedback, angry customers and potential returns to deal with. When editing photos, be sure not to use filters or anything that can mess with the product's look. You're not going to get points for having a 'vintage looking' product photo; you're going to get backlash. So be very careful and focus more on showcasing the product in a more realistic way that the camera may not have captured in the raw image.

6. NEVER Sacrifice Quality

If you believe having something is better than nothing, even if that something isn't high-quality, let me just burst your bubble. *90% of online buyers say that photo quality is the most important factor in an online sale* (Bruiet, 2019). There is no room for sacrificing quality, don't cut corners or accept that a DIY job is the best you're going to be able to do.

Even if you're doing it yourself in a limited capacity, there are ways to do it right. We don't recommend a budget approach to this step, but it isn't impossible to achieve great results if done well enough.

7. Don't Overload Customers With Images, Find a Balance

While you want to leave no room for mystery when it comes to your product, there is such a thing as too much. This "too much factor" can be quantified based on the number of product photos you have per product. For example, let's say you're a pretty prolific candle maker with a wide range of items. First off, kudos to you! Secondly, you need to be strategic about how many product photos you throw at customers. The line between a good amount of information and an overwhelming amount is thin, and you need to walk it like a tightrope. Aim for a consistent number of images per product, and try to keep it under five. My sweet spot is three per product, but four is still in the realm of acceptance while five is sometimes borderline.

8. Make Your Images Interesting To Look At

I want to make it clear that I'm not saying you need to go crazy here. There's 'interesting to look at', and then there's 'what am I looking at?' Things such as lighting techniques, editing tricks, backgrounds, angles and settings will add to the overall quality of the image. *78% of online shoppers want photographs to bring products to life* (Bruiet, 2019). Armed with this statistic, you need to work to make your photos work for your ideal customer. Always take caution in this part of the process, as being extra is far easier to achieve than perfection.

9. Allow Your Customers to Explore Your Product Photos

An interesting stat from Adobe Scene 7 (2014) found that *91% of individuals want to turn products around in full 360° spin.* This desire for an interactive shopping experience remains in high demand. It will likely only get more intensive as technology evolves.

People aren't fans of surprises when they're relating to something they're parting with money for. *22% of products sold online are returned because 'items look different than the photos'* (Nesbitt, 2020). As a result, they want to see the product from all angles and the 360° product view is a great way to achieve that. You're providing everything you have to help your potential customers make a well-informed decision about what they're purchasing.

10. Make Sure Your Product Photos Highlight the Benefits

When people see your product images, they want to understand how they could benefit from using the product. So while you have to show multiple angles of the product to see the product itself, consider doing live shots of people using the product to explain why it can be beneficial. Remember what I said earlier about selling a lifestyle? Well, this is a big part of that, using your photography to show why they need the product instead of just wanting it.

Avoid Making These Common Product Photography Mistakes

You know what it is and why it matters, but now it's time to learn more about what takes product photography to the next level. There are ten mistakes to avoid for better product photography.

1.Low-Quality Product Photos

If you believe having something is better than nothing, even if that something isn't high-quality, think again. *90% of online buyers say that photo quality is the most important factor in an online sale* (Bruiet, 2019).

2. Dark or Shadowy Product Photos

Customers want to see your candles, not need a candle to even see your product. When you're taking the photos, ensure that you have adequate lighting to fully showcase the product so that people know every curve, point, marking, and color that the candle comes in. People need to know what they're looking at and not fill in the image with guesswork.

3. Bad Composition

Using a larger product photo size on category pages increased sales by 9.46% (Bruiet, 2019). The moral of the story is don't go and create images filled with empty spaces and have a product that only takes up 50% or less of the total image size. 'Bigger is better' (High School Musical, 2008). Sharpay wasn't talking about product images and their composition. Still, she knew a thing or two about grabbing attention, so listen to her. Fill the picture with your product and display it in full force. The smaller you make it, the less confidence people will have in it, and when someone says size doesn't matter, know it's a lie. It's always a lie.

4. Unnecessary Elements

Let's imagine you've got a fun and quirky name for your candle, so you decide to do a product image with the thing that the candle was named after. As a consumer, they might get confused and make an impulse purchase thinking they bought chocolate. Instead, they just purchased the Chocolate Delight Candle that smells like chocolate. People make quick and poorly thought out decisions all the time, don't give them a window of opportunity because they will take it.

5. Unrelated Images

I wish I didn't have to say this, but if the internet has proven anything, it's that people don't always make logical decisions. If you're selling something, make sure you use images of the product and not of something that doesn't have anything to do with the product you're selling. For example, you're selling candles, so don't put a picture of wax as your product image. This isn't a before and after type of situation; nobody cares what the candle was before it was a candle.

6. Ignoring The Packaging

Don't ignore your packaging. Great packaging can really seal the deal on your company aesthetic so show it off by including an image with both the product and the packaging it comes in. Take pride in what you've created from start to finish and let people see it all on display. Sometimes the packaging can be that final determining factor that makes people hit the 'add to cart' button.

Pro Tip:

> Outsourcing product photos might be your best move if you're looking for quality results. This is because professionals have invested money into expensive equipment, software and have built a substantial knowledge in the art of product photography.

You can find some exceptional product photographers and freelancers of all types on Fiverr. Spend some time to explore their collection of product photographers and test the waters before making a firm decision.

Key Takeaway

The key takeaway should be this stat right here; *75% of online shoppers rely on a product photo to make a decision* (Bhatoa, 2021). So you need to take the concept of product photography seriously and ensure you present the best version of your product online for people to see. You're selling online where there is no shortage of things to buy; standing out is difficult and falling into obscurity is easy. Great product photos alone won't make you stand out, but standing out is next to impossible without them.

Chapter 3: Leveraging Etsy and SEO to Drive Sales

Twenty years ago, we wouldn't be talking about SEO (search engine optimization), let alone Etsy, but times have changed, and we have to evolve with them or risk getting left behind. With e-commerce becoming a primary source of consumer shopping and growing rapidly year to year, it's time to embrace the internet and all the potential opportunities it has to offer you and your customers.

Right now, *21.8% of the world's population purchases products online* (Bruiet, 2019). To put that into perspective, that's a little (relative to thousands of people) over 1.66 billion people. Human people, or as I like to call them, 'potential customers.'

So why do people like to shop online? In all honesty, you might have the answers yourself as you've probably experienced shopping online before! Still, here are a few reasons why online retail is growing in popularity as expressed so eloquently by this article in Tough Nickel (Jain, 2021);

1. The internet presents consumers with the '**24/7 Mall.**' They can get to a store in a few clicks, stay as long or as little as they like, and shop.

2. Comparing prices means consumers can find the best deals without traveling to multiple stores or dealing with numerous sales clerks. This provides **freedom of choice** and the **potential for savings** which is so valuable to consumerism.

3. No need to worry about **transport,** this comes up a lot when people discuss the benefits of shopping online. However, knowing you can do it from the comfort of your couch in your PJ's is appealing to most, if not every, consumer.

4. The **convenience** of online shopping can't be understated. Instead of worrying about the crowds, you can focus on shopping while finding out if Ross and Rachel really were on a break. Instead of waiting in line, you can enjoy the lack of lines on the way to the fridge. I don't know about you, but I think I might just take a 'day of retail therapy' myself.

5. Have you ever gone shopping only to find the product you want is out of stock? Well, if you're like me, you're about ready to rage before you remember you're a civilized person living in a civilized world- well, mostly civilized world. Online shopping doesn't present out-of-stock as much of an issue as brick and mortar stores do. That's not to say it doesn't happen at all, but it's far less frequent, and you can easily get notifications when items are back in stock.

6. The complete and utter satisfaction of feeling like you just saved some money when you spend

enough for **free shipping** is the rush shoppers crave. You feel like you just beat the system, saving a few pounds, dollars, or euros on your order getting to your home. The validity of that logic aside - let's say it's true, to avoid feeling guilty about how much we just spent getting that 'free shipping'- most companies provide either free shipping in general or at a small monthly fee. For example, a big proponent of this is the behemoth known as Amazon. Their Prime Service offers free shipping on almost all the products available on their website.

All of these reasons why online shopping is popular don't mean that brick-and-mortar stores have no upsides. Some consumers actually prefer them, so nobody is saying abandon in-person selling (*which we'll get into depth on in Chapter 8*). The idea is to diversify and innovate your business to meet the masses where they are, and many of them are online. Whether we love it or hate it, that's where they're shopping.

In this chapter, we'll explore Etsy and your own website to see how you can leverage them to work for your business.

Etsy

If you've never heard of Etsy, let's change that. Etsy launched in 2005 and has grown into a global marketplace for creative products. The types of products you'll find on Etsy are usually handmade, rather unique, collectibles, vintage treasures, and more. As time's gone on, Etsy has grown in popularity and ballooned in revenue. In 2020 alone, they were one of the companies to benefit from the

Covid-19 pandemic seeing a nearly 110.86% sales growth (Wall Street Journal, 2021). The insanity in that fact alone should be making you question why you're not on Etsy. If you are on Etsy but haven't seen results, you should ask why you weren't a part of that immense sales growth.

Before I explain how you can utilize and optimize Etsy, let's look at some of the pros and cons of this e-commerce marketplace platform.

Pros and Cons

Here are some of the pros and cons associated with setting up shop on Etsy.

Pros

- **Great if you are new to selling**

If you're new to selling, then Etsy might be a great place to start. Etsy is a great way to reach customers and offers an easy and quick way to set up an online store. Etsy is trusted and reliable. These will serve your business well as people won't question too much about your brand's authority.

Additionally, there is no favorability with Etsy. For example, suppose a customer searches for a very specific type of candle. Well, good news, your candle has just as much a chance of being found as someone who's been on the platform longer. It's not a guarantee; however, it's not at all impossible.

- **Free***

Anyone can enjoy the benefits of Etsy, especially as you can set up shop for free. You are not required to pay any design fees, hosting or domain fees, or anything else that might come up. This is not to say there are no fees, but the initial setup is 100% free.

- **Setup is easy**

Building on the free setup is the fact that setting up your Etsy store is incredibly easy. It's pretty much built to go, and all you need to do is list your products, and you're ready to start making some money.

- **An abundance of tools for sellers**

Etsy has many tools to make a seller's life easier. You'll have access to monthly sales statistics, social media tools, and they even host various tools by third parties. Sadly, some of these third-party tools may require a nominal fee to use.

- **Ads are easy to set up**

You can set monthly budgets for your advertising on Etsy. You can also create very specific ads depending on your goals. This helps boost product exposure and can result in a ton of sales.

Cons

- **Bad communication**

I'd be remiss if I didn't mention the shocking communication that Etsy is so widely known for regarding their customer service. My experience was consistent but was the worst kind of consistency. I

either received a response within 3 or 4 days or not at all. Sadly the latter was the more common outcome. As a seller, this can be infuriating. Thankfully there is a community that is far more helpful than some of Etsy's own representatives are. Additionally, you can always ask our amazing Facebook community of candle business owners, you can find us on the link below.
www.facebook.com/groups/candlemakingbusiness101

- **Hard to be found/differentiated**

The honest truth is that Etsy is a double-edged sword. On the one hand, you've got access to a large customer base and you can get found incredibly easily if people are searching for what you're selling. But, on the other hand, you're in a marketplace that is overpopulated with similar products, storefronts and creatives. As a result, getting noticed can be highly challenging. Furthermore, there's not much that can be done in terms of differentiation between you and a competitor.

- **You're not building a brand**

The honest truth is, people who shop on Etsy might as well think they're buying from a shop named Etsy that produces the products listed. There's very little evidence to support that any consumer who frequents Etsy even knows who they're buying from. That's not to say this is everyone. Still, I can confidently say a majority of the buyers on the platform simply don't pay attention to this at all. You'll need to insert your branding into every possible area to clarify that you're behind the product and to build brand loyalty.

- **You have to pay a fee per listing**

While zero setup fees are great, that pro sours quickly or simply fades from memory the further into the process you get. When you suddenly see the numerous fees Etsy will charge per listing, that free listing aspect will matter less and less.

- **You aren't in control of your own store**

This shouldn't come as a surprise, but it's still worth mentioning that using Etsy means you don't actually own your store. There is very little that you can do to set your store apart from another store in terms of aesthetics. Everything is essentially standardized, while the only difference in look and feel comes directly from your product images and products themselves.

Another critical aspect of not being in control is that Etsy could disappear tomorrow and everything can evaporate with it. When you're beholden to one platform that doesn't offer secure longevity, then a simple policy change can be enough to take you down. So don't put your candles all in one basket.

How to Optimize Etsy

There are 15 strategies that I've found work wonders to guarantee you make sales on Etsy. Many of these strategies rely on search engine optimization (SEO) to increase your chances of being discovered.

47% of Etsy traffic is through direct search (Pengue, 2021); therefore, it's so important to understand how you can alter or set up your Etsy store to facilitate growth.

1.Keywords

Keywords are what help get your products found in a vast ocean of options when someone searches online. Keywords are what allow for relevant information to answer users' search queries. When creating your listings, you want to make sure all your keywords relate to your products. For example, if the candle is in a tin, then 'candle tin' could be a keyword. If it smells like a pinecone, 'pinecone candle,' 'pinecone scented,' and 'pinecone scented candle' are all relevant keywords.

Avoid jargon and any confusing language when crafting your keywords. These won't be useful and will lessen the chances of your product being discovered.

When crafting keywords you need to focus on long-tail keywords. Long-tail keywords are more specific search phrases that narrow down search results using a combination of keywords to describe the product. For example, 'soy wax body candle' instead of just 'candle.' People who search online usually start very broad with their search before narrowing it down continuously to find exactly what they're looking for. This can be the difference between a sale gained and a sale lost. You may be thinking, how will I ever get sales if long-tail keywords are less searched? It's true, they are less searched, but they still get a lot of hits, from people who are further along the buying process, which means they are more likely to buy. Therefore, there are a lot of benefits; you are more easily found and, if you are found, they are more likely to buy from you. It's a win win!

2. Intentional Word Order

When a product is shown in a sea of products, the importance of your listing titles first three words becomes crystal clear. Etsy favors the first couple of keywords, so you are more likely to show up if someone searches them. Additionally, many people shop on their phones, and the first three words on the listings are the only ones which are shown, therefore, they need to be highly relevant.

3. Improve Etsy Quality Score

An Etsy Quality Score (QS) improves when a buyer clicks or favorites, or purchases from your storefront. The higher your shop's score, the higher you rank on a page.

You can improve your Etsy quality score in multiple ways, but customer reviews are one of the most powerful methods available. Reviews act as social proof that your product is worth purchasing (unless those reviews are negative, of course). So find creative ways to elicit reviews from customers who’ve bought your candles, examples are:

- Thank you notes
- Reaching out via email
- A discount for a review
- A giveaway for anyone who leaves a review

Pro Tip:

> Never ask for a 'positive' review in 'exchange' for something as this is against Etsy's policies. What you can do is ask for an open and honest review and try to explain how grateful you are and how much reviews help your business.

Additionally, adding new products consistently to your store shows that you're active and thriving, which Etsy wants to see from the store on their global marketplace. Etsy favors active store fronts, as it wants to show new products to its regular shoppers, so they are constantly seeing different things and are not bored, therefore, keep shopping on Etsy.

Finally, tag your location as this will expose you to people in your area. Etsy often promotes stores based on location and does push local stores to customers.

4. Make Your Photos Stand Out

All that talk in Chapter 2 about why product photography matters has brought us here. There's no substitute for good product photos when it comes to selling online. Etsy isn't going to promote a store that has product photos taken with a terrible camera, poor lighting, and a lack of effort. Considering this is one of the only chances you get at differentiating yourself from your competitors, I'd hope you take this step seriously!

5. Fill Out As Many Attributes As Possible

Make sure you explain every aspect of your product in the product description. Ensure there's no confusion or mystery about what your product is made of, its height, width, weight, where it comes from, and anything else necessary. The more information you give to a customer, the less likely they receive something different to what they had anticipated, increasing customer satisfaction and the likelihood of them leaving a review and being a repeat buyer.

6. Sales & Promotions

You want to embrace sales and promotions as a means to entice people to purchase your products. Like I always said in 'Candle Making Business 101' everybody loves a discount! Getting a customer to try out your product through a promotion means they might buy that product, or other products from you later after all offers have expired.

7. Competitive Shipping

If possible, provide free shipping. People love the word free as they immediately associate it with saving money or getting more value from a purchase. I've often bought something based on the concept of free shipping, as even I'm susceptible to thinking I'm saving money. In hindsight, I don't know how much I truly saved, as it's likely the cost was absorbed into the overall price tag, but that doesn't matter. What matters is my initial thought and the fact that I acted on it to ultimately purchase the product. That's what you want to target, that gap in thinking which doesn't last forever. If you can't provide free shipping, make sure it is competitive, as no one wants to get to checkout and realize it will cost an extra $200 to ship!

8. Focus On Etsy Ads

There are two types of Etsy ads;

- Cost Per Click - You pay when someone clicks on your ad
- Offline Ads - Etsy advertises your product on other platforms like Facebook, Instagram, etc. You only pay for this type of advertisement if your product is bought using the advertisement link. The downside of offline ads is the relatively high finder's fee Etsy charges (15%).

Before we start, it is important to know how Etsy decides on ad placement. Your spot is determined by a number of factors, the main being your quality score and your budget.

When starting out, I do not recommend running ads to your store, you need to build up some reviews first or you will end up wasting your money. I recommend only running ads 1-2 months after your store opens. When you do start running ads, I recommend spending $3 - 5 a day for at least a month. You can then gather enough data from this to optimize and improve your ads.

Take note that Etsy enrolls you in offline ads from the moment you join the platform, and if you don't want to be a part of offline ads, you'll need to opt out. However, I recommend staying enrolled as there is no initial fee. In the beginning, this can help you more than it can hinder you.

9. Improve Your About Section

Your about section does matter despite what you might think. Try to write something informative, fun, engaging, and enjoyable. You want to showcase your brand's personality as you're not just selling your candles; you're selling an experience to customers on Etsy. Furthermore, a well-written about section can spark the interests of the press and open the door to an interaction that might lead to greater exposure.

10. Review Your Analytics

Analytics offers valuable insights into what is working, what is selling, where you're succeeding and failing. These results can drive critical decisions such as which products to promote more, which products might be poorly optimized, and so on.

Pro Tip:

> Always promote your best products as you are more likely to see a greater return on investment (ROI).

11. Link Your Etsy Shop on Pinterest

So two exciting stats to know; 89% of users are looking for purchase inspiration, and 50% of users go to Pinterest specifically to shop (West, 2021). These are insane statistics that just highlight the need for you to link your Etsy store with your Pinterest account and take Pinterest seriously as a social media platform (More on Pinterest in Chapter 6).

12. Constantly be in the Mind of Your Customers

You want to find ways to constantly remind customers that you exist. The most effective way of doing this, in my eyes, is through the use of email marketing. You'll be able to use the weekly newsletter as a way to remain front and center in the minds of your customers and foster a relationship with them that can span years. Instagram and Pinterest are other ways to connect with your customers and showcase your products. It's said that it takes a consumer seeing your product seven times before they're willing to even commit to a purchase. That's insane, but all the more reason to showcase your brand and expose potential customers to your candles at every turn.

13. Interact With Your Customers

When it comes to interaction with your customers, you want to focus on;

- Responding quickly
- Conducting polls and surveys
- Replying to comments (if possible all of them or a vast majority of them)
- Showing your face.

Nobody trusts faceless brands. They want to see the personal touch; you are the personal touch!

14. Use the 30 Hashtag Slots You're Given

Hashtags are essentially the SEO component of social media platforms. They help push your images out to more people and foster engagement from users who stumble upon your post. This can help increase your following, and that can lead to an eventual sale. Of course, hashtags won't automatically make a post successful. Still, it will widen the net and expose it to more people giving it a fighting chance (more on Instagram marketing and hashtags in Chapter 5).

15. Influencer Marketing

Influencers, like it or not, hold an immense amount of cultural power and relevance. They could sell fire to a forest, and in some cases, they might as well be doing just that considering some of the random things they promote. Finding, pitching, and securing an influencer can dramatically increase traffic to your Etsy store and this could result in sales. Most influencers have thousands upon thousands of followers. That's a ton of people who, in all honesty, have likely never heard of you or your business.

It's not enough to implement these strategies and then just walk away. You've got to treat everything you do with SEO as ever changing. In response, be dynamic and open to change to meet the algorithm's needs. Think of the algorithm like the plant from Little Shop of Horrors. The more you feed it, the bigger it gets, but the bigger it gets, the more it eats. So the algorithm is constantly telling you, 'feed me, Seymour!'

The good news is that the algorithm can go 3-4 months without being fed (unless there is a major update) before you'll need to go back to your setup strategies and reassess and reconfigure.

www.yourwebsite.com

A website is something that sooner or later you're going to have to do if you're a brand looking to be taken seriously. A website is one of the criteria for running a professional and successful business. In a world that's increasingly transitioning to existing online, allowing your business to get left behind is not an option.

Pros and Cons

Here are some of the pros and cons associated with setting up shop on your own website.

Pros

- **Shop can be completely personalized**

You are in control of how your website looks and functions. Considering one of the cons of Etsy was an inability to customize your storefront, this is a massive benefit.

You can find various ways to differentiate your storefront from the numerous competitors in your niche and find a way to be the best option for all their consumer needs. But more importantly, you can do this in style.

- **So many apps (mostly on Shopify) if you want extra features**

Through third-party plugins, you can improve your website in so many different ways by adding new features and tools to make it easier for people to shop on your website. Of course, it's essential to be careful as there is such a thing as overdoing this aspect of your website. Still, if done effectively, you can create a winning experience for your customers. User experience is so important for building trust and making more sales. The easier or more personalized the experience it is for a customer to checkout, the better.

- **Can buy own domains**

When people shop on your website, it's your brand's name that's everywhere and not Etsy. As a result, you've got more authority and brand recognition because all your website viewers are exposed to is your brand.

Cons

- **Subscription fees**

Websites require monthly subscription fees to keep everything running. This is in addition to transaction fees and advertising fees. It's difficult to say if a website is more expensive than Etsy overall because, in some cases, it could be that it still works out cheaper.

Etsy has been known for its intensive fees across the board. So while subscription fees aren't the greatest news, they might not be the most detrimental con of taking on this online opportunity.

- **Hard to get noticed when you are first starting**

In the beginning, you'll find it takes a while to actually get noticed online. You'll need to implement effective SEO to be discoverable and constantly promote your website at every available opportunity. This is a stark difference from Etsy, where you can get discovered by chance.

- **Harder to build and get used to**

Etsy is ready to go from the start, and that's just not how a website works. You've got to build your website from the ground up, and that can take a long time to achieve. Additionally, you've got to consider where you're going to build your website. These additional steps mean it's a much more intensive process than Etsy.

Which Platform Should I Use for My Website?

The three options you should be considering when it comes to platforms you should use for your website are Wix, Shopify, and Squarespace. Of course, each one of these options has its pros and cons, but you've got to establish an understanding of what they offer and how they might suit your business's online needs.

Wix

Starts at $23

If you're a smaller shop just starting out then, Wix might be the best option for you. It's easy to navigate, affordable, has no transaction fees, and has excellent customer support. However, one of its most significant downsides is that it's got a basic inventory and analytics system. Hence, growth isn't its strong suit.

Features Include;

- Unlimited products regardless of your chosen plan
- No transaction fees
- Payment options available include Square, Stripe, PayPal, and Wix Payments.
- Easy-to-use drag-and-drop editor
- Built-in ability to sell on Instagram

Shopify

Starts at $29

Suppose you're looking for a place to start your business to grow it exponentially. In that case, Shopify is the perfect platform for you. It's a bit more on the pricey side than Wix and does have transaction fees, but it's well worth the money. The only real downsides to Shopify include its need for a third-party app for multiple currencies and the fact that if you switch templates, it means reformatting your entire website.

Features Include;

- Unlimited products regardless of your chosen plan
- 0-2% transaction fees

- Payment options available include Stripe, PayPal, Apple Pay, Amazon, and Shopify Payments.
- Easy-to-use drag-and-drop editor
- Built-in ability to sell on Instagram, Facebook, and Pinterest

Squarespace

Starts at $18

Squarespace is known for offering a well-designed ecommerce builder with the potential for making some stunning sites. Additionally, Squarespace offers flawless in-depth features. For example, it offers social media integration, inventory system, and analytics tools, just to name a few. It's not as expensive as Shopify, in terms of its monthly fee. However, its transaction fees are, in some cases, a percentage higher. In addition, it's lackluster when it comes to payment and shipping options and can be rather challenging to scale.

Features include;

- Unlimited products regardless of your chosen plan
- 0-3% transaction fees
- Payment options available include Square, Stripe, and PayPal
- Best design of any e-commerce builder
- Built-in ability to sell on Instagram

I personally recommend using Shopify, as it has so many apps which you can easily integrate into your website, many of which are free. These can massively help your customer experience, which I think is one of the most important aspects of a successful business. You need to try to make your customer feel special at every opportunity!

DISCLAIMER: There are obviously a lot more website platforms out there, I recommend doing your own research before committing to a platform to make sure it is the right fit for you.

Google SEO: How To Drive Traffic To Your Website

There are so many ways to achieve effective SEO through both organic and paid methods. However, suppose you're going to pay to get results. In that case, I recommend trying to optimize organically first, and here is how!

Organic

Many organic SEO methods can help drive more traffic to your website. Here are some of the most effective ways to achieve organic growth;

- Promote your website on your social media through the use of the bio section of your profile.
- On Pinterest, link images back to product pages or helpful blog posts on your website.
- Ensure on-page SEO requirements are met. This will include things like:

- **Headers-** have the best long tail keywords to help you get found.
- **Meta descriptions-** these are backend descriptions, make sure they relate to your candles, to help you rank better on Google.
- **Image alt-text-** make sure you describe your photo with long tail keywords in the alt-text section.
- **URL-** ensure your URL is clean and understandable.

- Target the right keywords and long-tail keywords.
- This is more for the techies of the group...Implement schema microdata practices into your website. Scheme microdata makes it easier for Google's army of search engine bots to locate and index your pages. The result can be better rich site snippets that might entice people to visit your site.
- Make sure your site is fast, easy to navigate, and responsive. Don't leave any room for frustrated visitors as they'll jump ship quickly, which will negatively impact your website's bounce rate. A negative bounce rate isn't good for SEO as Google takes this as a sign that your website isn't meeting the browser's needs.
- Invite guest bloggers to share their expertise with your audience. They will likely share the post with their audience, boosting traffic to your website from an untapped audience.
- Interview industry thought leaders and post it to your website. This leads people searching for the

interviewed thought leader to your website. Additionally, you're boosting credibility and brand recognition.

- Include your website link, product pages, or blog posts as calls to action in your email newsletters. (More on email newsletter in Chapter 7).

- Create a community on Facebook and engage with them to ensure they feel like it's a safe space where creatives can connect. The payoff is that you can utilize this community and share links from your website to the community and get them to visit the site, which drives up the traffic. Even if they don't buy anything, the increased traffic boosts your appeal to Google's SEO bots. I've created a community on Facebook and have found tremendous success in doing so!

- Interact with your customers wherever the opportunity arises. Let them know they're being heard every step of the way!

- Keep an eye on all the metrics available to you and improve in any areas where it's clear an improvement is necessary. Google has a lot of tools that can be installed onto your website to help you understand what they want from you in terms of site functionality, speeds, and discoverability. Tools such as Google Site Kit can be installed on your website and provide you with constant communication with their helpful services. Other notable services include;
    - Google Search Console
    - Analytics
    - PageSpeed Insights
    - Optimize

    - Tag Manager

- Voice search optimization is the process of researching long-tail keywords and then providing answer-focused content optimized for snippets. This can be useful if someone asks Siri, Alexa, Bixby, or any other smart device to answer a question relating to your topic. They might pick your answer and read it out, which can drive people to view more information and your products!

- Visit aggregator sites and submit relevant information from your website (through the use of links to said relevant information) as the answer to people's general questions. Think of sites like Reddit and Quora, for example.

- Include numerous quality backlinks to websites that contain a great deal of authority. For example, if you're talking about 'Ten Best Apps for Candle Makers,' include links to their App Store/Play Store pages.

- Take old content and constantly update and repurpose it. So, for example, you can take the post, 'Best Instagram Candle Makers of 2020,' and update it for 2021, and then again in 2022. This is a process known as 'Historical Optimization'.

- Include social media share buttons so people can easily share content they find interesting with their friends and followers on social media.

- Make sure your website is compatible with all devices. There should be an increased focus on mobile user interface (UI) as most people these days view websites on their phones especially if they are coming directly from a social media platform.

- Make quality customer service a priority. 42% of customers said they have bought more after a pleasant customer service experience (Patal, 2020).
- Explore and attempt to get media coverage and press relations to drive traffic to your website (more on media coverage and PR in Chapter 7).
- Know what you're talking about and be a topic expert/leader.
- Get friends and family to share your website with their following. It's free, and if they loved you, they'd do it. So don't be afraid to use that line.
- Explore the idea of creating blogs, videos, and a podcast to reach new audiences. While I don't have any idea what a candle podcast would look like, I'd be lying if I didn't say I was intrigued.

Paid

If you've done most of the organic SEO options and want to crank it up a notch, then it's time to put your money where your mouth is and utilize paid ads.

- Advertising using Google Ads. You set the budget, define the goals of the ad, optimize it using relevant keywords, and let Google do its magic.
- Leverage Google retargeting ads and focus on the people who've already visited your website to try to lure them back.
- Chase referral traffic through the use of influencers (More on influencers in Chapter 5). You can track the performance of each referral using unique codes.

- Use BuzzSumo or similar services to determine what your competitors are up to and what content is driving traffic. This can give valuable insights as to how you can potentially steal some of that audience away through your own content.
- Use services like Crazy Egg to see where exactly you're losing and gaining visitors. This kind of tool can help you replicate the success of well-performing pages while fixing pages that are driving away visitors.
- Use tools like Ahreds and SEMrush to further explore and define your SEO to optimize every last page of your website. These services will provide you with a roadmap as to how you can improve your overall traffic.
- Plaster QR codes on your products packaging, flyers, posters, purchase 'Thank You' cards, and have it link back to your website where they can rate the product they purchased. In the case of flyers/posters, find your store more conveniently.
- Run contests or giveaways that rely on your website being shared or a purchase being made, etc.
- Offer time-sensitive discounts that require immediate action.
- Run ads on the major social media platforms with the goal of getting people to your website.

While this list of possibilities is likely overwhelming, it's actually very easy, for the most part!

So The Big Question...Etsy or Website?

In my eyes, I don't see any reason why it shouldn't be both! Of course, I realize I can't just say that and leave it as is. I need to give you some determining factors that might better answer the question.

1.Where Does Your Target Market Shop?

If you're selling something aimed at men, I have some terrible news… Etsy isn't going to be where your target market shops. Women overwhelmingly make up the clientele on Etsy, while a website targets whoever you set it to target through the use of keywords, content, and products.

2. Your Budget

If you're cash strapped, especially in the beginning, then focus on Etsy and Instagram marketplace. Save your cash and then build your way up to a website of your very own.

3. Your Goals

What are you hoping to achieve with Etsy and a website? Define your goals for each and determine if you need both options. In my opinion, if you can afford it, a website isn't negotiable. While I advocate for using both platforms, I think if one had to go, it would be the one where you've got less control and are charged numerous avoidable fees.

4. Available Time

If you don't have the time to throw into a website, focus on Etsy and Instagram Marketplace instead. A website can be a demanding undertaking, especially when you're getting it off the ground.

Key Takeaway

There are a lot of opportunities on Etsy and your own website. You can not only grow your sales but also establish a reputation and fast-track your brand awareness. Take every advantage you can to ensure you're getting the entire worth of these two excellent means of marketing your business. Get email sign-ups, social media follows, likes, sales, reviews, and whatever else you're able to get!

When marketing your business online, you want there to be a place to go. A place where your product can be found, considered and purchased. Both options offer a level of authority, credibility, and exposure. The key is to understand and utilize the free and paid options to expand your reach. The goal is world domination. Sorry, I misspoke. The goal is to connect with customers, maximize exposure, and sell like candles are a scarce resource!

CHAPTER 4: TIKTOK IS NOT A TREND IT'S A BUSINESS' NEW FAVORITE TOOL

Have you heard of TikTok? At this point, I'd be worried if you hadn't! This social media app has become a favorite for billions of people who've embraced the short-form video content platform. If you think TikTok is going anywhere, I have something to tell you… it's not. You need to seriously consider using this platform as it can help your small business go viral and you can break into younger markets. It's also just a lot of fun, hard work, sure, but fun nonetheless.

This chapter will break TikTok down and explain why this is becoming a favorite tool amongst businesses for marketing opportunities. But, more importantly, I'll explain how you can make it on TikTok! So, let's get into it.

Did You Know;

TikTok may have graced the internet in 2016, but it wasn't until 2019 that things really took off for the social media platform. Below are some incredibly interesting facts about TikTok. Read each of these carefully and try to think about how your business could benefit.

1. TikTok has one of the highest engagement rates in the United States when it comes to influencers. Their engagement rate is 18%, while platforms like Instagram have 3.86%, and YouTube has 1.63% engagement. It's pretty easy to see this dramatic difference between these various platforms. It only underlines the fact that TikTok should be taken seriously and it is a great outreach and marketing tool for you, your candles and your brand.

2. The average TikTok user spends 850 minutes a month on the app. For context, this equates to nearly half an hour a day. Furthermore, the study found that 9 out 10 users visited multiple times throughout the day. I know I'm one of those 9 people who simply can't get enough of the app! Its intuitive AI (Artificial Intelligence) means the algorithm is brilliant at tailoring content purely for my tastes. This can work in your favor, as the app does this for your ideal customer too. Therefore, if your videos appeal to your target audience, your sales could end up going through the roof.

Average daily social media usage is nearly 2.5 hours (2hr 29 mins to be exact). TikTok equates to 1/5th of this time, claiming an average of 28 minutes per day. This high time percentage shows why TikTok is essential for business growth.

While Snapchat remains the most popular social media app amongst teens at 34%, TikTok has claimed the second position with no intentions of slowing down.

3. In 2020, TikTok became the most popular overall app downloaded in the world. It was also the 2nd most popular app on the Apple Store. On the Play Store, it was the most downloaded app in March. Overall, TikTok became the third Fastest Growing Brand of 2020.

These aren't easy metrics to hit for an app. But, for TikTok, there was simply no stopping it. In the United States alone, 89 million people downloaded the app in 2020. In May of 2021 alone, TikTok was downloaded more than 80 million times!

4. As it stands, TikTok has the highest social media engagement rates per post, with entertainment ranking as the most popular category based on hashtags. The app's Daily Page Views amount to 1,000,000.

5. 63% followed someone in the last month, 54% commented on a video, and 43% uploaded a "duet" video. When people duet your video, they're sharing it even further and engaging with their audience through commentary.

6. TikTok has over 1.1 billion active users worldwide. In China, the app has 600 million daily active users. These numbers aren't slowing down, quite the opposite, actually. Worldwide the app is continuing to grow exponentially.

7. When you look at age groups for TikTok users, you'll see where things get even more interesting.

61% of U.S. TikTok users are women. This is good news considering women are most likely your primary target market when selling candles. Having access to such a large audience means there's a ton of opportunities to sell your candles with the power of TikTok pushing people towards your brand.

Of all TikTok's monthly active users in the U.S., 32.5% are between the ages of 10 and 19. Furthermore, 29.5% are aged 20 to 29.

69% of U.S. teenagers are regular TikTok users, with 29% of teens considering TikTok their favorite social media platform!

8. Love or hate this fact, but TikTok is the most popular social media platform for kids at 41%. Children aged 4 - 15 average a whopping 75 minutes per day on the platform alone!

Geyser, W. (2021, September 28).

Why Should My Business Bother With TikTok?

Numbers don't lie. TikTok's overall performance, engagement and popularity mean a great deal of potential can be found, explored and utilized on the social media platform. Brands rely heavily on social media to connect and understand their target audience better. Below are more facts which highlight the important role of social media marketing and how you, like larger brands, can benefit from heavily focusing and constantly improving your digital marketing approach. Again, read each of these carefully and try to think about how you would market your candles most effectively.

1.69% of Marketers Use Social Media For Brand Awareness

With TikTok retaining so much of its user's time and attention, why wouldn't you want to be one of the brands vying for just a slice of what's available? TikTok is such a massive platform that there is room for everyone to benefit from the powerful social media platform. You can improve your brand's online presence faster on TikTok than on almost any social media platform currently available. This is primarily due to the algorithm which works to create tailor-made content delivery to its users based on their behavior in real-time.

2. 59% of Marketers Use Social Media to Understand their Target Audience

You must market your candles to a specific target market, and you must try and understand their demographic as much as possible. This includes everything from how they speak, to what they love, to what they do for work, then you need to create content based around these ideals. 49% of marketers use social media to develop creative content because there's no better place to get ideas than the source.

With TikTok, you can determine what sounds are popular and tailor your videos to fit that sound. In addition, you can see what trends are popping off and try to incorporate them into something relating to you, your brand, and your product.

3. 52% of Marketers Use Social Media To Increase Web Traffic

The main idea with any social media is to hopefully take social media users and turn them into customers. First things first, you need them to get off of TikTok and onto your site. The more you can engage with users, the more likely it is that you'll get a portion of them to venture to your site and potentially to a sale. It's like leading a horse to water or a Gen-Z to candles.

4. 43% of Marketers Use Social Media to Increase Community Engagement

A ton of marketers are using social media primarily to engage more easily with their customers, whilst driving sales. Suppose you were to venture onto TikTok. You'd likely come across a video where the average user showcases how a brand commented on their video with something humorous or snarky. This further increases your brand's awareness. Want a good example of this? A TikTok star named Emily Zugay recently went viral on TikTok for creating some of the worst logos for well-established brands as a joke. Do you want to know what happened? Some of the biggest brands in the world engaged with Zugay and asked her to make them a logo before they took it a step further. Countless brands changed their professional logos to Emily Zugay's joke logos. Some even went as far as to send PR packages with the logo plastered everywhere. It was unlike anything I've seen, and it's a pure example of the power of this app and its connection abilities with consumers.

5. 46% of Marketers Use Social Media to Grow a Brand's Audience

People want to be loyal to brands. It can be intentional or unintentional, but that doesn't change the reality of the statement. The benefit of having an audience means your reach becomes easier to achieve, and sales can be boosted as a result. Imagine making a video of you actually making your candle, showing the process and your skill. Now imagine a few thousand people reacting to this video out of the hopefully millions who watched it. What's going to happen is that your initial video will get millions of views (hopefully). This could create a positive knock on effect with more and more people being exposed to your brand. Even getting thousands of people is powerful, so don't get wrapped up in a word like a million.

6. 44% of Marketers Use Social Media for Promoting Content

Marketers use social media to promote certain campaigns or content. They often boost these campaigns through paid ads to help it reach more people that maybe wouldn't have seen the content organically. There's absolutely nothing wrong with this. However, when you are first starting out, I'd recommend trying the organic route as much as possible especially on TikTok as it has far greater organic reach.

7. 57% of Consumers Follow Brands To Learn About New Products and Services, with 47% Wanting To Stay Engaged With The Brand and Any News On the Brand

You want to hook viewers and have them follow you because they feel it's necessary to keep up to date with what you're doing. The more people are interested in your brand, the more likely they will become customers or remain loyal ones.

8. 49% of Consumers Unfollow Brands When Customer Service and Product Are Of Average or Below Average Quality

The internet is a fickle place, and once you've lost someone, it's tough to get them back. You can't go onto TikTok and show off a product not even worthy of a DIY video. Don't showcase work that you're even a tiny bit unsure about, as you don't want to lose the audience you've worked so hard to achieve in the first place, or worse, tarnish your brand right out the gate.

9. 91% of Consumers Visit Brands Websites or Applications When They Follow Them on Social Media

Interest in a brand often leads to deeper dives, and that's why consumers go from social media to a brand's websites to explore a little more of what the company offers and to make sure it's not a scam. So hooking in a potential customer and making your social media so great that they *have* to follow you is a must. Especially, as 89% buy from a brand if they follow them on social media.

Geyser, W. (2021, September 28).

TikTok Strategies

Now for the exciting stuff, strategies to help you succeed on TikTok. The best advice I can give you is be consistent. This is a quality that is prominent in all social media platforms. Consistency is favored as you're almost building trust with the algorithm. While not every video will land up being a hit, you'll find that a handful can really surprise you with the reach and numbers they achieve.

Beyond consistency, here are some of the ways you can make your content more appealing.

#Hashtags

When you're posting a TikTok, you're given 150 characters to do with whatever you please. One of the things you can throw into this space is hashtags. You must use it! Before you go crazy and use all the most popular hashtags, take a step back. You need to be targeting hashtags that are under 200k views (not 200 million views) when you are first starting out. I know your candles and content will be great, but competing for attention in an overcrowded hashtag is like thinking the lead singer in a band is going to see your 'marry me' poster at a concert and take you up on the offer. Is it impossible? Not at all. Is it difficult as hell to achieve? Yes, it really is.

To locate hashtags that work for your niche, you need to become an investigator. Searching around TikTok for hashtags that work for you and your content. A good example is if you type in candles, #candletok comes up first as this is the most popular hashtag in the candle niche. Click on this hashtag, then go through each one of the videos that used that hashtag and take note of other hashtags they are using. Make sure you check how many views each hashtag has. If it is way above 200k views then don't bother using them just yet. When your hashtags are too large you probably won't be discovered at the top of that hashtag and therefore it probably won't aid your video reach, so it's pointless. Another way to find hashtags is to type in one hashtag into the search bar. Then click on the hashtag's tab on the right hand side and scroll through similar hashtags, again taking note of their view count. Make sure you write all the potential hashtags you could use down for easy reference later.

Always, and I mean always, make sure the hashtags you choose are relevant to your video and, where possible, your niche. Sometimes you'll have to go experiment a bit outside your niche depending on the video, but don't use a hashtag like #santa while making a candle shaped like a bunny.

Finally, make sure the hashtags you're going with will actually be sought after by your target audience. It's great that Kevin, the skateboarder from Long Island, found your TikTok, but how valuable is this interaction? Is Kevin going to buy a candle? Is Kevin going to follow your candle business? The answer is probably not. When your hashtags are too broad, so is your audience. That's great in theory, but as the saying goes, 'when you appeal to everyone, you end up appealing to no one' (Hill, 2016). You want to be careful not to miss the people that actually care about your candles; something tells me Kevin is not one of them!

I have compiled a list of relevant hashtags that could work for you and your content. Please check these hashtags first before using them as view count can change;

#etsyseller

#mysmallbiz

#smallbusiness

#candles

#decor

#candlecompany

#candletok

#smallbiz

#candlebusiness

#smallbusinesscheck

#candlemakingbusiness

#etsycandles

#asmrpacking

#asmr

#candlemaking

#packingorders

#candlesoftiktok

#smallcandlebusiness

#aestheticcandle

#candlewax

#candleaddict

#candlelight

#candlediy

#candlehack

#candletrick

#candlelove

#candleburning

#candlelover

#candlescience

#homemade

#smallbusinessowner

#etsy

Please note that these are just generic hashtags for candle-making, and they're not a guarantee! A great way to research hashtags and create a hashtag collection is to use software such as flick.tech, which is only $7 a month but is extremely powerful at sourcing relevant hashtags. A bonus is that you can use it with Instagram too!

Pro Tip:

> Go to the top eight hashtags in your niche. Then, within each of these hashtags, comment on the top ten videos within that hashtag. Make sure your comments are engaging and not just copy-paste responses. TikTok isn't going to appreciate 80 comments all saying, 'that's so cool!' It's not going to be 'so cool!' when you get shadowbanned. I guarantee commenting will help boost your views. Try and do this as often as possible.

Content

When it comes to content, you're going to want to post roughly three to seven videos a day. I know, it sounds like a lot but trust me you'll live. You might even thank me for this advice!

You're going to need to come up with ideas for your content, and here are a few to get you started!

- **BTS (behind the scenes)**
  - Day In The Life Of A Candle Maker (or whatever else fits the Day in the Life of video model)
  - Making
  - Packing
- **Collection Review**
  - Best Creation
  - Worst Creation
  - Weirdest Creation
- **Your Brand**
  - About You
  - Brand History
  - Brand Origins
  - Brand Story
- **Vibey Videos to Nice Music**
- **Satirical Content Relating To Your Line of Work**
  - Reenactments of Funny Customer Interactions
  - Strange Orders
  - Strange Requests
  - Candle fails
- **Aesthetic Videos**
  - For example; a video of you burning your candles
- **Customer Reviews/Feedback**

Pro Tip:

> What's content without solid trending music choices? That's right, it's content that doesn't go viral! You're going to want to use trending music to reach as many people as possible. Use the TrendTok App to find up and coming and trending sounds, it also suggests different hashtags to use with those sounds. This app is a must have and such a time saver!

How To Succeed On TikTok

If you're looking to make waves on TikTok, you need to nurture your presence on the platform. Ensure you're doing an extensive job of reaching new people wherever possible. TikTok success includes brand awareness, sales, and a stronger customer community. These are all benefits that are worth fighting for, but it doesn't have to be so tricky! Here are some tips and tricks to help you find success on TikTok.

1.Know Your Target Audience

Going into TikTok not knowing or understanding your target audience isn't going to translate into solid results. In order to connect with your audience, you need to understand who you're targeting and then relate and connect to that audience through your content and engagement strategies.

The goal should be to educate and entertain your audience, not the entirety of TikTok's user base. Less is more, and in this case, targeting people who might actually be interested in your business and products is more effective than trying to market to every user, in every country. It doesn't matter if you think Kevin (yes, we're back on Kevin) from Long Island is a challenge that you're going to crack. It's not a connection you want to make because it will not serve your brand.

2. Create Evergreen Content

The number one goal when creating content should be to make it as evergreen as possible. You want your content to be accessible and relatable for years and not just for a day or a week. Of course, as I said before, some of your content will not be evergreen (e.g. if you are jumping on a random trend), and that's fine, but if you can find a balance, you'd be better off for it.

3. Always Hop On Trends

TikTok thrives on trends. If you're creative enough, you'll find a way to utilize the trends and tailor them to your candles. As a result, not only will you likely reach more people, but you might end up with some unique content that stands out. For example, having a successful video based on a trend can be one of those game-changing moments for your business. As a result, you could gain a lot of traction and, hopefully, followers and customers. Another benefit of hopping on trends is that you're showing a more personality-driven side to your brand. This matters as people can connect more with you on a social level which can be a gateway to retaining their attention and hopefully getting their patronage.

Pro Tip:

> Use a trend app or website to help me see what is trending on TikTok and find all the sounds that are rising the ranks. It's a quick way to cut out all the unnecessary research and just get straight to doing the trend yourself. Again I recommend using the app TrendTok for this.

4. Create and Get Involved In Challenges

Similar to trends, challenges are another popular aspect of TikTok and can help you get a lot of traction. You can participate in challenges and even attempt to get some of your own going. Again, it's crucial to find popular challenges which your target audience may watch.

5. Educate Your Target Audience

Provide value to your audience by educating them on things they never knew, e.g. the art of candle making. In between your more humorous videos, the trends, and the challenges, throw out videos that speak to the finer details of the craft, tips and tricks, and best uses for your candles. For example, you could have videos like;

- Benefits of your certain type of wax
- How to Properly Cut Your Wicks
- How You Can Reuse/Repurpose Your Vessel - a plant pot or a pencil holder/make-up brush holder.
- How To Reduce Stress - use one of your candles as an example
- The Perfect Date Night Picnic Set Up - talk about what you need and mention your candle as a must-have.

6. Hashtags

I've already touched on hashtags, but some things are worth repeating. You need to find a way to use hashtags effectively to make it easier for your audience to find you.

Never use random hashtags, and instead, use ones you know have a chance of connecting you with your target audience. Additionally, you're going to want to combine branded, trending, and business-specific hashtags for the best results. Consider it the hashtag trifecta!

7. Cross-Promote

TikTok is great, but it's not noble to be TikTok exclusive. Marketing simply doesn't survive in a vacuum. Suppose you focus all your efforts on one social media platform. In that case, you're not only ignoring the entire contents of this book (bar a chapter), but you're also doing your business a disservice. You MUST cross-pollinate your videos if you want to see meaningful results.

In my early days of TikTok, I was only getting a measly 150-250 views per video. That's not the kind of results you want to see. That same content posted to Instagram was bringing in 4000 views. However, bear in mind my followers on Instagram weren't that much better than they were on TikTok. The difference is that it was found by more people on one platform and resonated with them.

Repurpose your content to Instagram (as a Reel), Pinterest, and YouTube (as a short) in that order. If you don't think you can manage all these platforms realistically, cut from the least important but never cut Instagram. In my eyes, that is a non-negotiable for cross-pollinating.

Pro Tip:

> Before posting a video made using TikTok to other platforms like Instagram, be sure to use the Snaptik.app website to remove the watermark! Instagram gets a little offended when they see you just recycling your content to their platform. The algorithm is the equivalent of a mean girl trying to keep you down. So don't end up in Instagram's 'Burn Book.' It's not a fun place to be ever.

8. Remember the Importance of Timing

You won't get this step right for a couple of weeks as it takes time for your analytics to start showing results, so don't beat yourself up over it. Review your analytics and see what timings work best for your audience. Then post your videos at their most active times. This is not a one time jobby, you need to keep fine-tuning your posting times until you get the best results. Review your timings roughly once a month to make sure your posting times are still relevant for your audience.

9. Engage!

TikTok is first and foremost a social media platform, and that means you sort of have to be somewhat social. The best approach for engaging with your audience as much as possible is more simple than you think. Commenting is, first and foremost, the easiest way to connect with other creators. Secondly, duets. There are people on TikTok who've become famous purely due to the duet/stitch aspect of TikTok. This is when they take your video, showcase themself next to your video in a stitch and react or comment on it. You can do the same thing. For example, if a customer gets one of your candles in the mail and does an unboxing, you can stitch and comment on their video.

No matter what you do, avoid being spammy with generic comments or over liking because TikTok is stringent regarding its community guidelines. Unfortunately, they're not the greatest at fair or equal enforcement, so avoid being spammy as you don't find out if you're one of the few that gets your account banned, even temporarily.

10. User-Generated Content

User-generated content is one of the most effective ways to spread the word about your brand. This is when customers make content based on using your candles, or engaging in challenges you've set, it's almost as if you've got an unaffiliated marketing team! When this starts happening, and it will trust me, you can use them for your own account. React to them and build trust in your brand while engaging with your followers and, in this case, customers specifically. This is an instant raiser for legitimacy as social proof is one way everyone can see that there is no scam or falsehood when it comes to what you're selling!

Pro Tip:

> Why not put a note on your thank you cards that if they post about your product on social media and tag a specific hashtag (something branded) then you will DM them with a unique 15% off code? This encourages customers to be more interactive with your brand and you can use their content in your marketing strategies!

11. Always have a Call To Action (CTA)

Even TikTok needs a CTA! You need to include a CTA in every video you make and tell people to do something you believe is necessary for your current goals. It could be liking, sharing, commenting, following, or it could be going to your website to claim a deal. These all help with the algorithm as TikTok and social media overall only want to share content they know works. They're not looking for run-of-the-mill content. They want content that keeps people on their platform! A classic CTA is someone saying "follow for more tip" at the end of their TikTok whilst pointing at the follow button.

12. Be Creative and Persistent

Rome wasn't built in a day, and neither was a following on TikTok. So the more consistent quality you give the platform, the more likely your chances of winning the content lottery and getting a viral or semi-viral video. Conversely, if you allow the lack of results early on to cause you to give up, then you'll never know what could have been had you pushed through and created the best content.

TikTok Tips!

There are so many valuable ways you can leverage TikTok to your advantage. Here are some of the tips I've used to grow my profile, and so far, they've been working wonders!

1.After 1000 Followers, Shift Gears

Once you've managed to get your first 1000 followers, you need to start going live at least once a day. The best practice is to go live an hour after posting a video. In terms of how long you should be going live for, I recommend 20-45 minutes.

2. Utilize Greenscreens

Don't stick with plain and boring backgrounds. Instead, use a green screen and change it up a little. While you might be marketing your business, that doesn't mean you can't inject a little life into your content! Show off some of that award-winning personality you've got in abundance. If you don't have a personality, then dance or something. Charlie D'Amelio has over 120 million followers, and I highly doubt personality was the driving force behind this astronomical success.

3. Create Educational Evergreen Content

You want to create content that has no relationship to time, and what I mean by that is to make it evergreen. TikTok and pretty much any social media platform often throw content at you with little regard for when it was posted. Of course, not all your content will be evergreen. However, actively looking to make your videos relatable any time of the year gives it power compared to time-sensitive content. Additionally, make your content educational, this means people watch more of the video to learn which is favorable when it comes to the algorithm.

4. Make Entertaining Videos to Hook and Lure in an Audience

Don't think a short TikTok is all you need to get people to watch your content. TikTok has proven the power of a few seconds and the will of people to watch something throughout. Always keep in mind how the beginning of your content goes so that you can retain people's attention and make them stay right to the end. Suppose people are scrolling away after a couple of seconds. In that case, you're not producing content worth watching which means you need to completely reassess your approach.

Pro Tip:

> Make your captions hooking. For example, you could say '3 things I bet you didn't know about our candle jars'… then if a person wanted to find out the answer then they would have to watch all the way to the end.

5. Business Account To Creator Account

This is important, when starting out on a new account, use a business account before transitioning to a creator account. After you gain your first thousand followers, then you can transition back to a creator account. The reason behind the business account type at the beginning is so you can have a link to your website in your bio from day one, whereas you can't on a creator account. The major downside, however, is that you can't use certain commercial sounds. This limits how many trends you can create. Hopefully, it won't take long for you to get back to a creator account and can be a motivator to get you to the first 1000 followers!

How To Utilize TikTok Advertising

If you've mastered the more organic side of TikTok, then it's time to start using advertising tools to really get some results. The best tool to use is TikTok's Ad Manager. I do not advise using the promote button just yet, as it's somewhat unreliable.

So how do you set up a custom Ad?

Step One: Create Campaign

When you're setting up the campaign initially, you're going to want to target the ad's audience range. You can do this to age, gender, location, interests, and more. This means a strong knowledge of who you're trying to find is imperative to an ad's true success. You can also create custom audiences or lookalike audiences to reach people similar to your existing customers.

You need to ask yourself what the objective of this campaign is. Is the point to;

1. Increase traffic?
2. Increase the reach of your video and boost views?
3. Sell a product?

4. Gain followers?

Understanding the reason for the ad makes it easier to create and measure its success or failure.

Step Two: Budget

You've got three choices for budget;

1. Daily Limit
2. Lifetime Budget
3. No Limit

Make sure you take your time to figure out how much you are willing and able to spend on a campaign. Additionally, make sure the budget that's set, ends when it should if the content is time-sensitive. For example, you don't want Christmas ads running in January. You will not get the most for your money this way.

Step Three: Ad Groups

Every campaign can utilize ad groups to optimize your ads, all while measuring performance. When creating an Ad Group, you can choose the following;

1. Ad Placements; either manual or automatic.
2. Ad Details; includes promotion type, display name (which shows up on the ad), profile image, and 20 ad tags.
3. Ad Target Audience; you need to remember to target this ad from age to interest.

4. Set Optimization Goals & Bidding Methods. You need to consider how you'll be billed for the ad, for example, CPC (Cost Per Click). Set these bids and realistically tell the app how much a click is worth to you with the budget you have, and TikTok will work towards that budget set.

Now that everything is set up, it's time to start the ad. How exciting!

Step Four: Analyze & Track

There are many ways to track the performance of an ad. Before getting to the analytics provided by TikTok, a great way to follow performance is by linking the CTA success rate in terms of web traffic. For example, after posting a video calling for users to go to your site, did they? Another method is just using the TikTok analytics to determine the success of your ad from the source. There, they break it all down for you in the ad manager. Don't be afraid to adjust your ad based on the results, you need to constantly be learning and updating your ads to make sure they are optimized. Just be careful not to over-tinker, as it might backfire.

Pro Tip:

Recently a new ad type popped up on TikTok called **Spark Ads**. This ad type allows for using existing content from your profile instead of videos explicitly made for ads. You want to focus on content that's already proven successful. You're not looking to make a diamond out of coal. You're looking to turn a diamond into a diamond ring.

Key Takeaway

There is so much power to be found in TikTok if only you're willing to take on the platform headfirst. This app requires a lot of work to master, but if this book hasn't clarified how true that is across the board, you might need to re-read it! Be smart, creative, educational, and entertaining to win over an audience. Considering there are over a billion active users, I'd say you've got some room to work with to find just the right people.

Chapter 5: Instagram and Influencers- Selling a Lifestyle

Instagram is a titan of the social media industry. Behind YouTube (which I would barely call a social media) and Facebook, it's the go-to place for most social media users! It's also incredibly popular with a younger demographic, and that's why you need to get on this platform. You need to find a way to thrive amongst the millennials, gen-x, gen-z, ABC's, just all the people!

In this chapter, we're going to cover a lot of aspects of Instagram; from the basics, to influencer marketing to try and grow your account and boost your sales! Okay, let's get on with the behemoth of a platform that is Instagram.

Instagram Basics

There are a few basic things you need to know about Instagram if you're going to succeed on the platform. For starters, you need to have a business account in order to get Instagram Analytics which is necessary if you want to grow. It's straightforward to switch an account to a business page. Just go to your settings, and at the bottom, you'll have an option to change to the account type you require.

This is just a tiny part of what is ahead on your Instagram journey, but it's an essential first step.

Weekly Posting Guideline

On Instagram, schedules matter. You're going to want to try and post the following amount of times a day, or week depending on the type of post;

Feed Posts = 2 a week (Preferably carousels)

Stories = 5-10 a day

Reels = 4-5 a week

Use analytics to understand when the best posting times for your brand are throughout the day and week. You can learn when your followers are most active, and once you've figured that out, you should start posting roughly 1-3 hours before that time. So you want to try and target their most active time. By posting well before that, your chances of being seen during peak hours increase exponentially.

Don't forget to share on your stories when you have posted on your grid. You should include the following elements into your 'new post' story;

- 5-7 hashtags that are RELATED to your post
- Geotag the most relevant locations to your post

You'll want to hide both the hashtags and geotags under your photo/video to expand the post's reach. This method is an easy trick to help you produce more traction on your post.

Pro Tip:

> If you're making videos on TikTok - which you should be doing - then use websites like Snaptik.app to remove the TikTok watermark. Now you can post those TikToks on Instagram as Reels! Don't post videos with the watermark, as Instagram gets pretty peeved off when users do that.

Plan Your Feed

Your Instagram feed can't just be a collection of random images that share no relationship other than being on the same page. You need to plan your content and create a sense of cohesion amongst the posts. You're working with a grid, which means that your brand's structure and colors can be seen at a glance. Considering the focus on aesthetics regarding Instagram, you can't just throw content onto it without a second thought.

My favorite planning app for my Instagram feed is Planoly. I use it to place my content and plan my overall feed. This allows me to remain consistent in style and also saves me a ton of time and effort! An additional benefit is knowing what your content will look like next to each other to ensure it compliments before you post it on Instagram itself.

Planning your feed is an integral part of Instagram marketing, and far too often, it's an afterthought. Take what you post and how you post it seriously. You'd be surprised at how important this can be when someone decides over whether or not to follow your account.

Pro Tip:

> Try to follow a pattern to keep your feed consistent, for example a checkerboard.

Instagram Giveaways

Instagram giveaways are an excellent opportunity to achieve multiple results all at once! With giveaways, you can attract people to your page, grow your following, and create greater brand awareness! When figuring out what and how to do a giveaway, consider the prize and try to find other brands on Instagram of a similar or somewhat larger size who might want to join your efforts. A combined 'prize' across brands can benefit multiple businesses and reach more people.

Benefits of Instagram Giveaways

Here are several benefits of hosting an Instagram giveaway!

1.Build Brand Awareness

Want to get people's attention? Mention the words 'free,' 'giveaway,' 'win,' or anything along those lines, and you'll see a complete shift in the energy surrounding your page. If you craft your rules right, you can garner followers, comments, likes, shares, everything, and anything. This level of interaction will put your brand at the forefront of minds which would have never thought about your brand before.

Once the dust has settled and the winners announced, a fair portion of the participants might actually stick around. But, don't be disheartened when a lot of people unfollow after the giveaway announcement.

2. Increase User Engagement

Engagement matters more than followers. There. I said it. You can have a million followers but an appalling engagement rate. In that case, Instagram will treat you like you're not worth paying attention to, all because not enough people are paying attention as it is. With giveaways, however, you're creating a transactional relationship with people for a moment where they can potentially get something from you, but it costs their engagement to stand a chance. This boosts your standing with Instagram and can have lasting effects on how they treat your account in terms of importance.

3. Increase Your Instagram Following

You call the shots, you set the rules, and you can make one of the barriers to entry a requirement to follow your account. This will dramatically increase your follower count if you state ‘follow me’ in the entry rules (which you obviously will). For example, if you require people to tag friends, share the post, or other elements that get more people involved, then you can gain more followers from their friends' entries too. This is high-level user-generated content at work marketing your business for you!

4. Collaboration Opportunities with Influencers

Giveaways can be mutually beneficial for multiple parties involved, and this includes brands and influencers. You’re both after similar things; engagement, increased following, and brand awareness. Of course, you have an additional economic need and collaborating with an influencer or other brands can help you achieve that need. For starters, you’re reaching their following, which is likely substantial in comparison. Second, you’re getting the opportunity to reach new people in the process. Finally, some influencers have their ‘own’ product line or product that they regularly sponsor. This can be included in the giveaway, increasing the value.

5. Boost eCommerce Sales

Finally, giveaways can increase sales. How? Giveaways speed up the process of gaining access to Instagram’s eCommerce features. While Instagram’s eCommerce features are still relatively new compared to tried and tested platforms like Etsy and other online stores, the potential in this feature is notable.

Pro Tip:

> If you have a store already and run a giveaway, remember the ‘no purchase necessary law’ as asking participants to enter by purchasing something is forbidden.

How To Create an Instagram Giveaway

Step One: Pick a Prize

It’s excellent to consider running a giveaway, but what are you actually going to give away? Start thinking of prizes that you can do alone before moving on to find other people to join the giveaway with you. Examples of prizes you could use are:

- A candle
- A candle set
- Your new product launch
- Complementary products as well as your candles (e.g. the ultimate bath set- wine, bubble bath, your candle and more!)

Step Two: Craft the Criteria for Entering the Giveaway

Consider your goals for the giveaway and craft the rules around those goals. For example, if you’re looking to gain followers, make the requirements; like the post, follow the page, tag 3 friends in the comments and post this on your stories and tag us. Of course, not every friend that is tagged will actually do anything regarding the giveaway. Still, a lot of them will, and that can amount to plenty of new followers.

Other options include; signing up for your email newsletter, sharing the post to their story and following additional accounts (if other brands and influencers have been included in the giveaway).

Step Three: Decide How Long the Contest Will Run For

This can be tricky. Too long, and you lose steam, interest, and diminishing returns. Too short, and you don't get the full benefit of the giveaway and cut off many potential people who would have entered. Determining your giveaway's start and end date will be a challenge. It'll require considering the prize, the number of followers you have, your goals, the time zones of your most engaged audiences, and more.

Pro Tip:

When you are just starting out on Instagram, I would recommend having the giveaway running for 5-7 days.

Step Four: Create The Initial Announcement Post

Make a post-fitting of your giveaway! Make it stand out and include a strong image to serve as the foundation before showcasing the prize or text announcing the giveaway. Don't overload your photo with text. Instead, use the caption for the Terms and Conditions and entry requirements.

Step Five: Create Reminder Posts and Share Constantly

You're going to need to constantly remind people of the competition. So, you need to create posts you share every few days which can be related to your giveaway. Then, closer to the end of the giveaway, you can include the days left. The big numbers might really get some people moving, most people work better with a hard deadline!

Step Six: Choose a Winner

There are a ton of websites and apps to make this easier. You can just search for them and choose one that works best for you. For example, a popular choice is Comment Picker and AppSorteos. You simply copy and paste all your Instagram comments and copy it into the generator.

Step Seven: Spread the News of Who Won the Giveaway

Make the announcement of a winner an event. Hype it up, maybe make smaller prizes like gift vouchers for runners up and announce the winner with a dedicated post. You can also do the draw live, post a video, reel, whatever you want. Just make it something special and make it noticeable.

Instagram Trends

Always keep up with Instagram trends, why? Because Instagram's algorithm will favor your content as they want people to use their new features. Here are some new features you should be aware of and utilizing;

- Use new stories features such as the ‘add yours’ sticker.
- Use link stickers. Now you don’t have to have 10,000 followers to use links in your stories anymore, this makes it easier for people to shop your products even if you haven’t got ten thousand followers.
- You can now post from your computer. This makes it easier if you are using planning tools.
- **Reels**
    - You can collaborate with other people on Instagram reels, so it shows up on both of your accounts. Use this feature to collaborate with influencers or other brands.
    - Follow the same video guidelines which are in chapter 4 (TikTok), to make interesting and engaging reels.
    - Instagram is usually a week or two behind TikTok so try and stay ahead of the curve by using trending Instagram music. You can find trending Instagram sounds by:
        - Websites such as Tokboard.com
        - Go into reels, click the audio button and tap see more, these are sounds Instagram is

pushing so their algorithm will favor your post if you use them.

- Keep an eye out for the trending up arrow next to sounds, this implies the sound is up and coming.
- Listen out for sounds you hear a lot when scrolling through Instagram as they are probably trending!

  - Make your reels exciting by having cool transitions and different backgrounds
  - Make your videos engaging and evergreen.

There are so many trends and new features that are constantly being pushed out by Instagram. I recommend trying to stay up to date. The best way of doing this is following Instagram marketing experts on Instagram. My favorite is Catherine @the_marketing_club.

Marketing With Influencers

You might be rolling your eyes at the mere mention of the word *influencer*. Still, as a business owner, you should applaud their overhyped existence. Why? The facts don't lie!

- 75% of respondents indicated that they would be dedicating a budget to influencer marketing in 2021 (Influencer Marketing Hub, 2021).
- 49% of consumers rely on recommendations from influencers (Digital Marketing Institute, 2021)

- Brands earn up to $18 in earned media value for every dollar spent on influencer marketing. However, the average is closer to $5.78 per dollar spent. (Story Clash, 2021).

These stats, in combination with consumers' growing relationship with social media, matter. For example, in 2020 alone, due to the Covid-19 pandemic, social media engagement increased by 67% over average usage rates (Connect With Influencers, 2021).

What are Influencers?

An influencer is someone who has influence over someone else, usually due to their inspirational attributes. When I say inspirational, I purely mean that they live a glamorous life, or they make it appear that way. Then they sell that lifestyle on Instagram to millions of people. The concept is that an influencer influences others to buy things that can make their lives similar to their lifestyle.

Why Do You Need Influencers?

There are several reasons why you need to invest money in having your products promoted by influencers;

- They have credibility
- People trust influencers and trust what they're recommending.
- They have a large audience/following (generally, this is the case) however, I do recommend working with micro influencers too.

There are five types of influencers; mega, macro-influencer, mid-tier, micro-influencer and nano influencer. A mega influencer is one with over 1 million followers, a macro-influencer is an influencer with a significant global audience; anything over 500k. A mid-tier influencer is one with 50k to 500k and a micro-influencer has a smaller audience of under 50k. A nano influencer should not be undervalued, even if their followers are between 1,000 and 10,000 (mediakix, 2020). It's important to remember that followers, while important, aren't worth much if engagement is low.

Finding Influencers

To find influencers that are a good fit for your brand, you're going to have to do a lot of research. However, there are some great free methods you can use to locate the right influencers in addition to some paid ones.

Free Methods

Although it takes a lot more time and effort, you can find influencers for free. Some of the ways you can manually find influencers without breaking the bank are by;

1. Searching through your discovery page.
2. Searching for influencers you already know. Then you can go further by seeing Instagram's suggested follows based on that influencer you just followed.
3. Search through hashtags.
4. Search who your competitors follow.
5. See if an influencer already follows you.

6. Find by location tags. However, be warned that some influencers might just be on vacation and not actually from the area of the location tag.

7. Searching for articles on popular macro/micro-influencers and researching further.

8. Search Google for influencers by typing in 'your niche + influencers' and go from there.

Paid Methods

You can use numerous paid methods to find influencers and their contact details, the main being influencer databases. This is an easy way to find and contact influencers, however, an influencer has to opt into the database, so if you want a particular person then you may not be able to find them. Saying this, there are so many influencers out there, I am sure you can find the best ones for your brand, especially as most platforms validate their influencer status before adding them to the database. With an influencer database, you can filter by;

- Price
- Location
- Average engagement
- Followers
- Audience
- Demographics
- Top Hashtags
- Mentions

You can also contact, pay, measure results, and communicate with influencers via most of these platforms. Some of the platforms include; HypeAuditor, Indulance.co, and BuzzSumo.

HypeAuditor

Free/ $399pm (Pro)

With HypeAuditor, you can find some of the top influencers with exceptional authentic engagement rates. It goes further and breaks down what country the influencer is most popular in and what they generally post.

Influence.co

Free/ $600pm (Pro)

Influence.co is an influencer directory and makes it easier to find influencers by niche. Like with HypeAuditor, you can review engagement rates and various other stats.

BuzzSumo

Free/ $99pm (Pro)/ $179pm (Plus)/ $299pm (Large)

BuzzSumo has some of the best content research and influencer research tools for brands to use when searching for the right influencer and is significantly cheaper.

Deciding On An Influencer

To ensure you hire the right influencer, you have to consider things to see if they're a good fit for your brand and campaign.

1.Engagement

Suppose the influencers you've chosen have poor engagement. In that case, you should probably consider looking for other influencers who excel in this area. It's no good paying for an influencer who can't engage their audience! You probably won't see a good return on investment.

2. Authenticity

The last thing you want is an influencer who really comes across as an influencer. I realize how strange that sounds, but there are influencers out there that are natural, funny, somewhat down to earth. But, on the other hand, the Beverly Hills Barbie type influencers can sometimes lack authenticity, try to avoid these influencers, as people may think your product is unauthentic too.

3. Relevancy

Fame can come and go in a second. As a result, you need to make sure the influencer you choose has an online presence that matters. What I mean by this, is choose an influencer whose followers consist mainly of your target audience. There is no point working with an influencer whose followers are 80% male over 30, if your target audience is gen-z females!

4. Have They Worked With a Competitor Before?

Scan through their feed and search for a while to see who they've worked with before (some database platforms might have this information listed). See if they've worked with any of your competitors before and determine if this is a deal-breaker or not. If they've done so recently, you might not be able to hire them anyways due to exclusivity.

5. Macro or Micro

Do you want someone with over half a million followers or under? Micro-influencers usually charge less and actually have better ROI over macro-influencers. This is because their engagement is stronger than that of a macro-influencer with millions of followers.

6. Do You Think They'd be a Good Influencer/Ambassador?

There's not a chance you don't have a gut feeling when looking at the influencer, their content, their personality, etc. Ask yourself the serious question; 'would they be a good fit to represent my brand?'

Pre-Contact Agenda

You found an influencer; that's awesome! Now put down the phone, close the email, and hold on! You can't just contact them before anything is figured out about the overall campaign. Sure, you've probably done some preliminary work, but you need everything in place before actually reaching out to them.

Before reaching out to an influencer you should;

- Follow them on social media (from your brand account) at least 3 weeks before you reach out.
- Engage with their content! Like, comment, and share. If you can, tag them to get their attention. Don't be desperate but don't be too coy either.
- For a single campaign, you should aim to contact 20 influencers.
- Reach out 2-3 weeks in advance to allow time for;
    - A response
    - Interview
    - Make an offer
    - Sort through the campaign's details
    - Sign the contracts
    - Send the products for content
    - Allow time for content to be created.

Before reaching out, you need to handle campaign logistics and craft a marketing brief.

Sort Out Your Campaign Logistics

You need to figure out some crucial details regarding your campaign before reaching out to your desired influencer.

1. What do you want the influencer to do?
2. When do you want the influencer to do it by?
3. How much are you willing to pay the influencer?

4. Reach out to 20 influencers 2-3 weeks unless it's an extensive campaign, in which case send it well before the campaign.

5. Create and send a campaign brief.

6. Keep track of everything! Create a spreadsheet and include the following;

- The name of your 20 influencers
- Links to their social media profiles you want them to promote on
- Key Instagram metrics
- Notes you might have for yourself
- Dates you intend to make contact
- Dates you do make contact
- Dates you intend to follow up (if necessary)
- Dates you actually follow up
- Would you work with the influencer again? (Mark this off at the end)
- Campaign impact (If you used a unique link, track how that link performed and the metrics on their posts and your page, website, and store).

How To Write An Effective Influencer Marketing Brief

This might be one of the most important parts of reaching out to an influencer. You want to capture their attention, give them all the information, and leave no room for questions. So how exactly do you write an excellent Influencer Marketing brief?

1.An Introduction

Say Hello! Tell the influencer who you are, talk about your brand, your product, and any other relevant information they need to know about you to get adjusted.

Speak to these three points;

- Who you are
- What you want to promote
- Why they should be the ones promoting it

2. Compensation

Express what your intentions are surrounding compensation. Are you planning on paying them? If so, how much? If you intend to pay them in goods and services, be sure to express their value; however, most influencers respond better to monetary compensation.

3. Campaign Overview

Explain all the details of what you want;

- Where to post
- How much to post
- Things you want to be included in the bio and captions, such as branded hashtags, links, unique affiliate links, landing pages, etc.

- Campaign goals and key performance indicators (KPI)

Make sure your goals are SMART- Specific, measurable, actionable, relevant, time-bound.

- Express a desire to go long-term if you wish.

4. Campaign Deliverables

Explain in-depth aspects of the campaign, including;

- Brand guidelines
- The content you want to be created.
- Length of videos or stories (if necessary)
- Share talking points about the brand
- Dos and Don'ts.

5. Inspiration

If you have examples, then share them with the influencer to help them better understand what you want out of the campaign. Anything you can add for reference to make their lives easier and the content more to your liking should be included.

6. Deadlines

Make the influencers aware of all deadlines and timelines associated with the campaign. This is extremely important if you're advertising a product launch, rebrand, or anything significant.

7. Content and Results

To gain better insight into how the campaign did when it's all over, explain how you'd like the influencer to share links in their posts, stories, or anywhere else they might share it. Additionally, it is important to ask the influencer to share their statistics from the campaign with you afterwards, either from their stories or posts, depending on what you agreed.

Pro Tip:

> I recommend asking for their stats 24 hours after the post or story.

8. Content Usage Rights

If you want to reuse some of the content from the influencer on your own accounts, make sure you stipulate this as a requirement. Indicate what kind of rights to the content you'd like and discuss it with the influencer.

How To Contact Influencers So They Can't Say No

It's time to take the big step, reaching out to the influencers! You've been preparing for this, so you should be more than ready to contact your chosen influencers with confidence.

How To Style Your Messages

Before we go any further, you need to decide how you intend to reach the influencers. Personally, I think that the best way to reach out to an influencer is through email. If you're a small brand, a DM will look spammy and won't even be opened. If it is opened, I wouldn't expect a response. Influencers usually advertise their professional emails for business inquiries. So, look in their bio or see if they have a featured contact button at the top of their profile to get their email address.

Now that you know how to contact them, you need to craft a first, second, and third email. Here are some things to keep in mind when drafting your emails to your influencers.

- Make sure your subject line is catchy and can grab the attention of an influencer who's likely very busy. Keep the subject line under 40 characters, so the whole thing is seen on the phone, where most people read their emails. Experiment with an emoji if you're feeling up to it and see if this helps seal the deal and gets your email opened.
- Personalized subject lines with the name of the receiver can increase your email open rates by 2% (Super Office, 2021)
- NinjaOutreach achieved an 87.5% reply rate by using "I'd love to feature you in my post!" as their subject line (Grin.co, 2020)
- Make the messages as personal as possible. Mention content they've created, why you like it, why you think they'd be a good fit. Just provide some light convincing.

- Keep your emails brief. You won't get responses if your emails are pages upon pages long. Get to the point, be concise, all while being super friendly and personal. 50% of marketer emails are less than 300 words (Four Starzz, 2020).
- Be clear and don't make vague statements, offers, or declarations.
- Add a call to action for them to act. For example, you want to reply, so ask them to respond, letting you know if they can or can't do the campaign.

Reaching Out

Your initial communication should be friendly, informative, brief, and personal. Explain why this is beneficial for them, why you chose them, and throw in some compliments where you can!

Example #1 of a Reaching Out Email:

Hi [name],

My name is [your name] from [company name]. I've been following your [social media channel/blog] since [year/month].

I'm in awe of your approach towards [something they care about]. Your recent blog post about [post topic] really caught my attention and resonated with me.

I'm reaching out to you because we have a product that'll appeal to your followers. [Product name] is one of the finest [category of the product] in the market, and I'd love it if you would be willing to test and review it.

I'd love to send across a sample for you along with five others that you can gift your followers as well.

If you're interested, we can set up a phone call this week to discuss starting a collaboration.

Best,

[your name]

(Four Starzz Media, 2020)

Example #2 of a Reaching Out Email:

Hi [name],

I'm [your name] from [company name]. I recently came across your post about [post topic], and I loved your take on it.

We have numerous [name of niche (beauty, travel, etc.)] products that might interest you and your followers. And I wanted to check with you if you'd be open to working with us on an affiliate basis.

For every successful sale, we offer a flat [percentage]% commission. To make the offer sweeter for your followers, we'll provide a personalized 20% discount coupon as well.

I'd love to send across a sample of each product if you'd like to get started.

If you're interested, we can set up a phone call this week to discuss the collaboration that would provide value to brands.

Best,

[your name]

(Four Starzz Media, 2020)

Example #3 of a Reaching Out Email:

Hi [name],

I'm [your name] from [company name].

I've been following your [social media account/blog] since over [years/months] now, and you've scaled up quickly. Kudos for that!

I really admire the work you're doing for the [elaborate on a cause they support and talk about their work].

Our brand believes in [their cause] too, and that's why we strive hard to [uphold the cause (e.g. 100% animal cruelty-free products)].

I believe your followers will love our [product/service] and was wondering if you'd like to partner with us.

I'd love to send across a sample of our product for you to test and review.

If you're interested, we can set up a phone call this week to discuss the collaboration that would bring value to brands.

Best,

[your name]

(Four Starzz Media, 2020)

Pro Tip:

> After sending your initial email, DM the influencers you contacted and ask them if they received any communication from you. This means that your brand is more likely in their minds, but also they might go and check to find the email.

Following Up

Always send a follow-up email roughly 3-7 days after initial contact- this can sometimes result in a 53% open rate (Grin.co, 2020). You and your influencer may be in separate time zones. Therefore, your email might end up getting lost in the other emails they receive before even waking up. A follow-up removes the stress of them not seeing the original email. However, try and target sending the email closer to their time zone, not yours.

Example of a Follow Up Email

Hi [name]!

I'm [your name] from [company]. I sent you an email last week about [project] that I think could be beneficial for us to partner up on. I've come across your work on various occasions and really enjoyed [a project of theirs you enjoyed].

I thought you'd be interested in working on this project because [reasons]. If you're interested, I'd love to get your take on the project and figure out how we can make it beneficial for both parties.

Let me know if you're interested in working something out. It'd be great to get on a call on [day] or [day] this week at noon!

Just for reference, here are some projects I've worked on – just to let you know I follow through and am serious about making this work: [links to projects]

Best,

[your name]

(Grin.co, 2020)

Pro Tip:

> Use your automated mailing system to send emails to see when they have and haven't been opened. This way, you can plan your follow-ups around the open rates. If open rates are low across the board of all 20 influencers, try some A/B testing, test out different subject lines, and see what gains some traction. Additionally, try different times of sending the emails out.

Following Up On the Follow Up

Only follow up to the follow-up after 2 days have gone by without a response. Also, this is the last message you'll send. If you're still not getting a response, it's time to move on!

Example:

Hi [name]!

I wanted to check in one last time and make sure you don't miss out on [influencer marketing opportunity].

If you're not interested, no worries, but I would appreciate it if you could let me know!

Thank you,

[your name]

(Grin.co, 2020)

What To Do If…

- **They don't answer?**

Move on to the ones that did. This is why you need to contact 20 influencers. Not all of them will reply. You'll be lucky to get more than a 60% response rate.

- **They decline?**

Thank them for their time. Don't burn bridges and be rude or snippy. If it took them a while to respond, move on. Just say thank you and tell them you'd love to work with them someday. Keep the door open.

- **They are interested?**

Start a formal conversation where details start getting mentioned, and a marketing brief is sent. This is the time to see if you're a good fit, and if you are, send over the contract and start hammering out details.

How To Create An Influencer Contract

An influencer contract is a written agreement between you (the advertiser) and the influencer you've put so much effort into convincing to work with you. A contract is essential to make sure that both parties keep to their end of the agreement. Contracts reassure the influencer about your seriousness and credibility, but it also ensures you've clarified what is expected. With a contract, you're eliminating guesswork, creating a professional relationship, managing expectations, and offering yourself investment protection.

Here is what you need to include in an Influencer Contract;

- **Introduction**

The introduction should contain an overview of the entire agreement expressed within a few sentences. You'll need to detail;

- **Who the agreement is between** - you (the advertiser) and them (the influencer)

- **Where the content will be published (What platform? Multiple platforms?)**

This needs to be clear and concise. You'll get into more detail on specifics as the contract goes on.

- **Timeline**

Make it crystal clear when this agreement starts and when it is intended to end. If you've got specific dates for certain content, then outline that in detail. This can be announcing a product, special, or if you're asking them to post a series of posts.

- **Payment Terms**

Express how you intend to pay the influencer for their services. Either you plan to pay 50% upfront and the rest on completion, everything at the end of the campaign, on a pay-per-post, cost-per-acquisition or cost-per-click basis. Make the details clear, so they understand what to expect. Furthermore, express how you intend to pay them and request the necessary details of their account, Paypal, Venmo, CashApp, or whatever other payment methods they work with.

- **Content Requirements and Deliverables**

Don't leave any room for questions when it comes to what is required and expected. For example, express how many posts you require, any post guidelines you have, any hashtags you want them to use, let them know of any content approval processes, etc.

If you trust the influencer based on good word of mouth, past experience with them, or other reasons, you can give them free rein. This is just a risk you'll be taking, and whatever happens becomes your responsibility.

- **Things to Avoid**

Expressing what you want is necessary, but so is defining what should be avoided at all costs. This can be tone usage, word choices, product placement, etc. This again, guides the influencers and gives you peace of mind, that they aren't going to say something silly.

- **Copyright**

You may want to reuse posts made by the influencer at a later date on your own accounts. To do so, you'll need to claim content usage rights over the content created for your campaign by the influencer. They will retain copyright, but there will be an agreement set in place for you to access the posts for your own use after the campaign ends or during.

- **Cancellation Policy**

Suppose you're not happy with the content being made during the campaign, or you find yourself not enjoying the process of working with the influencer for whatever reasons. In that case, you need to craft an out of the agreement. You should also award the influencer the same opportunity. Sometimes professional relationships don't work out, and this can require a rethinking to the agreement. Negotiate this aspect with your chosen influencer after drafting your own proposal for termination eligibility.

- **Legal Responsibilities**

Your ambassador has a legal responsibility to follow the laws of the FTC (U.S.A.), ASA (U.K.) CCPA (E.U.), or any other applicable local agency that deals in consumer protection. Most of the laws concerning ambassadors are relatively similar, with the potential for slight differences. For example, sponsored posts must include declarations of sponsorship such as #ad or #paid. I think #ad is better. Something about #paid doesn't sound all that inviting from an outside perspective.

- **Confidentiality and Exclusivity**

During a campaign, you might supply the influencer with sensitive information regarding your business. Therefore, you want to include protection in your contract in regard to the handling of sensitive information. This includes what should happen to it after the campaign.

Additionally, you'll want to stipulate that the influencer can't work with direct competitors in your niche for a set amount of time, for example, 3 months.

How To Create A Brand Ambassador Contract

If you want an influencer to stick around long term and not just work with you for one campaign, then understand that means you want them to become a Brand Ambassador. This requires a different kind of contract than that of a once-off plug from an influencer.

Here is what you need to include in a Brand Ambassador Contract;

- **Exclusivity Rights**

Exclusivity rights stipulate that your chosen brand ambassador can't work with any direct competitors in the same niche, as this would create a conflict of interests. Beyond that, it would dilute the value of the ambassador, hurt your ROI, and damage your brand's image.

- **Repurposing Rights**

Influencers are usually consistent when it comes to the quality of their images. Considering they'll be creating content to market your candle, you'll likely want to reuse it. However, if you don't stipulate your right to this content in the contract, you risk being iced out. If you don't include it in the agreement you both sign, then the ambassador isn't in the wrong when they reject your content requests.

- **Deliverables**

Make it crystal clear what you are expecting out of this partnership. You will want to express requirements regarding;

1. How much content they'll need to produce in a week or month
2. What type of content should be created
3. Which social media platforms should it be shared on
4. What guidelines the ambassador needs to follow.

- **Approval Process**

Not every brand chooses to go this route as it can stifle creative freedom. Still, if you're very hands-on and have a strict set of brand guidelines, then an approval process might be something you want to add. This allows you to approve content before it's used. They create, you review, and finally, you approve or veto the content. This ensures that content is consistent, on-brand, and on message. Make sure you include how the approval process works within the contract. Don't make it vague.

What you could do is conduct a month-long approval process where you fine-tune the content if necessary and then allow for freedom beyond the month-long trial. This way, you've hopefully corrected mistakes, and your ambassador no longer needs the oversight.

- **Things to Avoid**

If you want your ambassador to avoid things when creating content, then make it abundantly clear within the contract. This can be anything from a phrase, set of words, tone, mention of competitors, etc.

- **Payment Terms**

Money is where the fights really take place. You want to be explicitly clear about what the terms of payment are in writing. This includes how much they'll get paid for their services and when they'll get paid. If you've got a bonus program for referral sales using a unique link or something like that, these need to be expressed in the same section.

- **Timeline**

You need to express what you expect regarding how many posts a day, week, or month you're expecting from your ambassador. If you have a specific schedule you want your ambassador to follow, then express this in detail.

Another aspect of the timeline you want to discuss is the length of the agreement. Are you wanting ambassador services for a set amount of time, or is it a rolling contract?

- **Cancellation Notice**

If you're on a rolling contract, both you and the influencer have the option of ending the contract. However, you can't just message one day and end it right then and there. You need to allow for notice of termination. It's similar to when you resign from a regular job, you have to give in your two weeks' notice. I'd recommend that for a brand ambassador contract you work on a month's notice.

- **Legal Responsibilities**

Your ambassador has a legal responsibility to follow the laws of the FTC (U.S.A.), ASA (U.K.) CCPA (E.U.), or any other applicable local agency that deals in consumer protection. Most of the laws concerning ambassadors are relatively similar, with the potential for slight differences. The main one that needs mentioning is the inclusion of '#ad' at the beginning of any sponsored post. This is non-negotiable and has to be included before every sponsored post.

- **Dos and Don'ts**

If any additional pieces of information fall under the dos and don'ts category, then mention them. For example, an obvious 'don't' would be blurry photos of the product. Nobody would enjoy this kind of content. It doesn't provide any real benefit and therefore shouldn't be posted.

Expressing dos and don'ts can decrease the chances of inappropriate or irrelevant content being posted.

Getting Influencers To Work With Your Brand

It's not difficult to get a great influencer to work with you as long as you follow these tips;

- Send a clear brief, and contract.
- Showcase great communication skills.

- Allow for some creative freedom. If your influencer has been doing this for a while, try and trust their approach. You can have the final say but don't watch over the entire process. There are significant downsides to content that fits too well inside a specific set of stringent guidelines.
- Pay fairly. Don't go cheap on an influencer. They are worth the money and not worth underpaying. You risk losing a great marketing tool if they don't take you up on the job because the price is too stingy.
- Remain consistent, and don't flake or prove to be unreliable.
- Don't tamper with guidelines after the contract is signed unless agreed in a collaborative problem-solving way with the influencer.

Pro Tip:

> If you find yourself confused about what is and isn't fair to pay an influencer, then use the Instagram pricing calculator tool from Inzpire.me. You can see the guidelines for pay very clearly here and make your own offer based on the information provided.

How to Get the Best Influencer Marketing ROI

You might be wondering, how do I actually get the biggest return for my investment? Influencer marketing is hard to measure, however, there are four ways you can ensure you get the best influencer marketing ROI;

1.Choose Relevant Influencers

Don't work with an influencer who is not relevant to your niche. For example, @Chadfisherman isn't going to sell your candles. I mean, he might… but I doubt many. Instead, find influencers who are as closely associated with your niches as possible, like interior decorators.

2. Know Your Influencers Audience

Review influencer's target audiences to ensure you're working with someone who is followed by your ideal target audience. You can find their demographics on influencer database websites and sites, but they're hidden behind paywalls. You can also ask the influencer directly for their media sheet which has their statistics before you sign the contract.

3. Work With the Right Platform

Facebook in general is for older people, Instagram for Millennials, while TikTok and Twitch are for Gen X. Know where to spend the most time to get the most out of your target market. For example, don't go to TikTok if your target audience is primarily grandparents!

4. Find Influencers Who Are Good At What They Do

Find the influencers who know how to work social media to their advantage, through telling stories in their content. When you find an influencer you like working with, you'll just know that's who you want creating content for you.

Metrics to Measure

It is always important to analyze the success of your campaign and influencer marketing. Here are some metrics to pay special attention to.

Revenue

The most basic way to calculate ROI is through revenue generated from the campaign. This can be flawed in the case of influencers. Their benefits are usually short-term (measured in brand awareness and sentiment, earned media value (EMV), and user generated content (UGC) with the potential for long-term monetary gain. That doesn't mean sales don't happen at all, thanks to the campaign. Still, it can be challenging to isolate revenue gains that originated purely from the campaign.

You can use link tracking or a unique discount code to determine roughly what sales were generated due to the influencer campaign. Industry benchmarks suggest that the average revenue generated is around $5.78 per $1 spent on influencer marketing which is pretty high (Inzpire.me, 2021).

Calculate ROI = (revenue generated/ investment)x100

Brand Awareness and Sentiment

Never base the idea of success on monetary gain. In the case of influencer marketing, some of the most successful campaigns result in a significant increase in brand awareness and sentiment. How do you measure that? You need to consider;

- Context of brand mentions throughout the campaign
- Positive, negative, and neutral mentions/comments
- Shares
- DMs

It's important to realize that brand awareness and sentiment can be the foundation to achieving monetary long term success as you can slowly turn followers into customers.

Earned Media Value (EMV)

Working with influencers is inherently short-term unless they become your brand ambassadors. In the short term, most of the results an influencer brings in aren't monetary. You will struggle to work out a profit from a single campaign as many have long-term gains. This is why EMV is so important. It allows a way to quantify the value of an influencer by considering the metrics they produced;

- Impressions
- Clicks
- Website visits
- Views

- Likes
- Shares.

Pro Tip:

Make sure you put in the contract, how you would like to receive the statistics from the influencer and when.

User-Generated Content

User-generated content is content that is created by anybody who doesn't work for your brand. It can be a customer, an influencer, or the press. You can repurpose these pieces of content on your social media, which helps aid the social proof factor of your business.

You can also calculate ROI based on user-generated content i.e., the cost of the campaign vs. the content you got out of it.

Intangible Metrics

Some returns can't be tracked the same way clicks, sales and impressions can. Here are some of the intangible metrics to consider;

- The buzz an influencer creates around your brand.

- The boost in authenticity and brand trust an influencer brings to your brand.
- Increased brand loyalty.
- Better relationship with the influencer and the chance to work with them again.

These types of intangible metrics live on and only get stronger. Other metrics may suffer constant fluctuation, but these only get more potent if you nurture them like a flame.

Mastering Instagram Ads

Influencers might be one of the best ways to increase brand awareness. However, traditional online marketing is still necessary to get maximum results. The best way to market your brand on Instagram is to use paid advertising methods on your stories and feed posts.

So how do you go about doing this?

Step One: Content

You have two options. Either you come up with new content to use for your ad, or you use content that's already been posted on your feed before the ad's conception. This is up to you. If you want to use content that's already been posted to your page, the process is very straightforward. Additionally, if you're not sure about what format to present your content, then utilize Instagram Ad Formats, which are free-to-use templates on offer.

Step Two: Campaign Setup

When setting up your campaign, you're going to want to address the following;

1. Target Audience
2. Budget & Time Frame

Understanding your target audience, your budget, and how long you want to run the ad will ensure it has the best chance of succeeding. Don't stretch a small budget over an extended period, as this will dilute the ad's potential reach.

Step Three: Track Performance

You want to keep tabs on how your ad is doing at all times. You can constantly amend certain items within your ad campaign to see if you can optimize ad performance. This is important as sometimes a minor tweak can go a long way. However, be careful not to overdo it, as you need to let your ads settle, and sometimes it will come with its own adverse effects.

Step Four: Cross-Promote

With the use of Ad Manager, you can make use of other Facebook-owned properties to further expand your reach capabilities. By allowing cross-platform promotion, you're advertising on two of the biggest social media platforms instead of just one.

Step Five: Start All Over

You've conducted an ad, you've learned some lessons along the way, now it's time to start all over again. The more time you spend using Instagram ads, the better you will become. Of course, it will take a while to fine-tune your ad recipe, but once you nail it, the results are going to be delicious!

Pro Tip:

> If you want to find out exactly who your target audience is, then check out my 'Customer Profile Cheat Sheet,' which you'll find in my book Candle Making Business 101. It's essential to remain up-to-date with your target audience as there's always the chance it can change. Always review your analytics to see who's interacting with your posts the most. You want to target your ads specifically to the people you know will pay attention to get a more significant ROI.

Key Takeaway

Instagram on its own, not that difficult. When you start adding influencers into the mix, the price goes up, the admin goes up, and most importantly, the sales go up! Don't neglect any element of Instagram, especially the use of influencers. This method of growing your online presence is loaded with benefits.

It is also one of the most highly effective ways to make some noise on Instagram!

Chapter 6: Pinterest and Selling an Aesthetic

Pinterest wraps up the trinity of social media platforms that you need to utilize to maximize your business reach and brand awareness. If you're unfamiliar, Pinterest is a place where you share images by pinning them to your own virtual pinboards. In addition, you can connect with other creatives, pin one another's content to your own boards and showcase your artistic abilities through sleek displays.

In this chapter, we're going to take a look at how you can utilize Pinterest to market your candle, grow an audience and hopefully make some sales!

Why Should You Use Pinterest?

There are so many reasons why you should be using Pinterest to market your candle business. For starters, they've got 454 million monthly active users (Statista, 2021). That's an insane number and it gets even better when you dig down deeper.

- 72% of Pinterest users are women (CED Commerce, 2021). Ladies love a good candle and you just so happen to be a candle maker. The stars are aligning. It might be fate.
- 83% of Pinterest users make a purchase after seeing a brand's content on the platform (CED Commerce, 2021).
- Pinterest is the fourth most prominent social media platform in the U.S (Pew Research, 2021).

Getting Started

If you're starting a new account, make sure you create a business account and not a personal one. If you're using a personal account, you want to turn it into a business account in the settings section. Now it's time to start setting up your profile.

Make sure you choose a high-quality profile and cover image to showcase a sense of professionalism in your brand. Finally, claim your website (in settings) to access analytics and provide an easy-to-access link to your online store.

How to Use Pinterest to Drive Traffic to Your Website or Etsy Shop

I don't even know how to stress this enough, but I will give it my best shot. Personal opinion, Pinterest might be the best weapon a creative business can have at succeeding. This platform has a tremendous amount of power to connect 'pinners' with your website or Etsy store. You've just got to do it the right way. Here are some of the many ways you can capture customers' attention and get them to click through to your website or Etsy store.

- **Pin at the Right Times and All the Time**

This will take a moment to master, but as you start getting into the swing of pinning content to Pinterest, you'll be able to figure out when is the best time to post. You can compare posts pinned at separate times through analytics to determine where the most activity is concentrated and when. As a result, you can tailor your content schedule to revolve around these times.

Pin multiple times a day, every day! I'd recommend posting pinning/repinning about 10-30 pieces of content a day. But, again, consistency is what the algorithm needs to take you seriously.

Pro Tip:

> 10-30 pins a day is a big undertaking and, honestly, a waste of valuable time. It doesn't matter how essential Pinterest is; you can't spend several hours a day looking for stuff to pin or repin. Instead, invest in a scheduling platform like Tailwind or Planoly to make this process far easier! You can get the free chrome extension to link your Etsy shop to your tailwind so you can pin your Etsy products straight through Tailwind.

- **Create Unique Images and Pins**

With billions of pins already on Pinterest, you need to look for any opening to be unique. I recommend creating images with a ratio of 2:3 (1000 x 1500 pixels).

Another step you're going to want to take is embedding strong images on your website before ultimately sharing them on Pinterest. This provides another direct link to your website and showcases your brand while adding to your credibility.

Another content idea is showcasing the various ways your candle can be used as a means of home decor or in general practicality. If Pinterest is just one big vision board, you've got to provide some of the vision and create inspiration through your pins. I know, that's a lot of pressure being put on a candle!

Pro Tip:

> If you are like me and aren't the best at Photoshop or other intense design platforms, you should use Canva. You can create stunning graphics and Pinterest-ready pins in seconds and in bulk! This will save you so much time as it's effortless to use.

- **Showcase Personality and a Little Bit of Humor**

Find a way to be funny and make a joke that fits your niche and has the potential to be repinned. For example, a customer review, but the reviewer is Harry Styles. The review reads, ‘this candle lights up my world like nobody else.’ Is it corny? Yes, of course. It’s a One Direction candle joke. You’re not headlining the Apollo, so quirky and corny are fine.

- **Include a Call to Action**

Guide your customers to your website or Etsy store by telling them to go there and providing the necessary links. You can advertise either option in a text overlay on your pinned image or in the pin description. I do a mixture of both, it depends on what the image vibe is, e.g. if it is a flatlay inspo pic then I would put it in the description.

- **Optimize Pin Description, Name and Business Description**

Speaking of pin descriptions, optimize yours! Focus on keywords and long-tail keywords. I will keep saying it no matter how repetitive it might seem. If SEO is a house, keywords are the foundation. Don’t bother with any other steps if you won’t take this step as seriously as the others! Okay, tough love out of the way, let’s get back to business.

With keywords in your description, you don’t want to just throw them in without a care in the world. Instead, you must weave them into the text like a conversation, with the candle as the subject.

Pro Tip:

> To find keywords, type potential ones into the search field and see what Pinterest auto-suggests. Building off your search, Pinterest then suggests similar keywords to complement your original searched keyword.

You'll also want to attempt to include keywords in your profile name, description and alt text. Think back to Chapter 3, everything you would do to optimize your Etsy or website, you need to do with Pinterest. Try to find a way to highlight your niche and put it on full display. For example, my profile name would be 'Grace Holmes- Candle Business Expert' (or something similar) not just Grace.

- **Test Out Variations of The Same Pin**

You never really know what is going to work on the internet. Just because Jane's Candle Shop is having great success with a minimalistic design doesn't mean you will too. You have to spend a ton of time messing around with different methods, strategies, content layouts, tone and pretty much everything. A great way to see what works best, try taking the same pin and crafting it in three different styles. You can obviously try as many styles as you want. Still, I worry that going more than three right out of the gate might be a nightmare administratively. Here are some examples of ways you can pin the same picture:

- Simple picture with no overlay text
- Same picture but with overlay text
- A grid picture made up of four images
- Different descriptions and alt text
- Create Boards

Take some of your candle business keywords and see what kind of boards you can create using those keywords as a part of the board's title. In the beginning, create 20 boards and populate them with other people's content. Once you've grown in impressions, following and interactions, then you can start posting your own content.

When it comes to the title of your board, while you need to use the keyword, don't make your title too long or short. Instead, make it relevant to the theme or purpose of the board. Furthermore, you'll want to use the keyword in the description as well.

Also, create boards for your products like 'Candle for Gifts,' 'Candles for Women,' 'Heart Candles,' 'Bubble Candles,' just get creative and specific in grouping your product pins in multiple boards. The general rule of thumb is to consider customers' search intent, this is what customers type into the search bar when they are looking for something. You need to ensure your boards are relevant and easily pop up in specific searches.

- **Make Use of Group Boards**

You can either join group boards, turn your boards into group boards, or both. To join a group board, you're going to have to look around Pinterest for boards to participate in within your niche. You can make this easier by using sites such as PinGroupie. Once you've found some boards you think are relevant you can reach out to the owner and tell them you'd like to be a contributor. Of course, you'll need to sell yourself and prove you've got something worth offering before they just let you join, so think carefully about your sales pitch. The other option is inviting people to join and contribute to your board which requires a lot of effort but is worth it if the board takes off.

- **Create an Aggro Board**

An aggro board should be the first board that appears in your collection of boards. It will be the board which features only your original content (candles). This acts as a quick and easy way for your followers to see your work specifically. You can showcase all your products in a sub-board to keep it organized such as, reviews, ideas, tips, tricks, whatever you want all in one place.

- **Grow Your Following**

Through consistent posting of quality content, you will grow in reach. If your content is worthwhile, it should attract followers. Growing followers should always be a priority. The more followers you have, the more impressions you make, leading to more clicks to your website or Etsy store.

Another method is following influential people in your niche and sharing their content to your boards. This can connect you with their audience. You can gain some traction by re-pinning popular pinners' most popular pins. This will also sustain relevant traffic for you.

Don’t be discouraged if things don’t go well for the first few months. It can take up to six months (sometimes over a year) to see actual results that are worth boasting about! Remember it is a marathon, not a sprint.

- **Cross-Pollinate**

Pinterest isn’t Vegas. This isn’t a ‘what happens on Pinterest stays on Pinterest’ kind of situation. Instead, you need to utilize content across the various platforms (e.g. Instagram, TikTok, Youtube Shorts) to save time, money, and effort. You’ll not only promote the content by sharing it everywhere, but you’ll allow it to be better seen by more people.

Another element of cross-pollination is generating backlinks to your website by promoting blog posts on Pinterest. These can, of course, be further shared on other social media platforms. Still, Pinterest is one of the best platforms for gaining an audience for a blog. This dramatically improves your SEO and generates traffic to your website.

- **Run Ads**

I’m going to get far more in-depth on the subject of Pinterest ads later in the chapter. Still, the bottom line is that they can boost pins and showcase you to the right audience if configured and run correctly. This can be a great way to get more sales from casual ‘pinners.’

- **Claim Your Etsy Store**

To claim your Etsy store, you’re going to want to go to the Pinterest settings > claim > Etsy and follow the instructions.

When you connect your Etsy store, you're turning your pins into shoppable pins. This means more rich data is being embedded into your pins, therefore, making them more valuable. Beyond that, you're creating a pin that's ready to be promoted, which opens the doors for more sales on that ad if the pin performs well.

- **Know Your Customer Profile Inside and Out**

Knowing your customer profile means you're able to create content that fits your brand's requirements without needing to refer to notes or give it much thought. The more you produce content, the more you'll understand your own brand identity requirements. This can include colors, language, tone, style, anything and everything that customers will interact with needs to be fine-tuned and recognizable as your unique brand.

- **Post User Generated Content**

Urge your customers to send pictures with your products. Select the most natural and alluring pictures and post them to your profile. For starters, free content! You get to hit your post quote without having to do any heavy lifting. Secondly, this creates social proof of purchase, use and enjoyment. This is a valuable asset to have showcased on your Pinterest boards.

Pro Tip:

> Don't forget to use a link, name of your shop, an icon, or anything that you can use for branding your pins. This will protect it

from being stolen or copied.

Focusing On Promoting Your Etsy Store

Suppose you're more interested in promoting your Etsy store. In that case, some of these additional tips might be extremely helpful in getting the most out of your Etsy/Pinterest relationship.

- **Add Price Tags to Your Pins**

Adding price tags to your pins will automatically include you in the gift section. This is a great place to be as you get further exposure to customers looking for things to purchase. Additionally, when you add the price, you also can link your Etsy store directly to the pin.

- **Offer Something Unique and Exclusive**

People are always looking for something new, unique and not widely available yet. So, the power of limited supply is genuine and you can take advantage of this to create a sense of hype around your Etsy store.

- **Create a Pinterest Community Around Your Etsy Store**

Don't be afraid of asking for things. For example, ask your audience to like, re-pin and post their own pins of your products and tag you in the pin on their boards. Create a community with your customers where this kind of thing is possible, and you'll find a lot of them are willing to support your business.

- **Share and Credit Other Creators**

Find creatives you enjoy on Pinterest and Etsy, share their content with your audience and tag that creator. When you give them credit and showcase what you've done, they might just reciprocate. Don't just do this for doing its sake. Make it authentic. Actually, appreciate what you're sharing. If you don't believe in a product but share it, you're fooling your audience more than anything else and you are creating distrust.

Pro Tip:

> A goal you should try and have is to get repinned by Etsy themselves. This would be a massive deal as it opens you up to a large audience of 10+ million monthly views.

10 Minute Growth Strategy

One of my favorite writers over on Handmade Seller, Laura Nightingale, designed and developed this strategy. Her Pinterest results are a testament to her incredible growth strategy, which I implemented last year and found highly effective! This is Laura's 10-Minute Growth Strategy (Nightingale, 2020).

Duration: 60 Days (Minimum 10 minutes per day)

The first thing you'll want to do is schedule your own pins that you've created outside of this 10-minute growth strategy. Post 8 - 10 of your own pins, then find 20-30 pins from other people to fill the rest of your day's content. Tailwind is one of your best bets at making this growth strategy a reality. Considering you'll be posting to a ton of different boards, you'll need a service that can keep up!

For pins, you can explore the creators you follow, and if you're struggling, just look at the suggested posts within the posts you've selected. With Tailwind, you can join boards and tribes to find content to repost. This is extremely helpful and time-saving so take advantage of this feature. If your goal is 30 a day, 10 of your own pins and 20 repins, then don't post more than that! Save extras for the next day's schedule.

This strategy isn't a guarantee. You could give it your best shot and still find it doesn't do anything for your following, impressions, or engagement. However, if it works, it more than likely will produce some absolutely insane results. Eventually, you'll get to a point where seeing a number that's expressed with the letter M won't have that same sticker shock it did the first few times you saw it.

Pinterest Ads

98% of Pinners say they've tried new things they found on Pinterest, versus 71% on other social media platforms (Hootsuite, 2019). The average profit per dollar spent by Pinners on advertising is $2, which is 29 percent higher than the average profit per dollar spent by non-Pinners (trend-online, 2021).

How To Utilize Pinterest Ads

Advertising on Pinterest is a lot easier than you'd expect. However, considering it's just another social media platform, similar rules apply to setting up and carrying out an ad on the platform.

1.Install The Pinterest Tag

Before running ads, be sure to install the Pinterest Tag. The promoted tag allows you to better see how your ad performs by tracking users' actions from your pin to your website. This includes signups, checkouts, and searches.

2. Decide on a Campaign Goal

Pinterest will ask you to select one of four goals for your Pinterest ad.

- Increase Traffic to Your Business Website.

You can acquire some really high-quality leads and send users to your website, and you only pay-per-click.

- Build Your Brand Awareness

Increase your brand's exposure with current and even prospective customers. You'll be charged per 1000 impressions.

- Increase App Installations (if you have an App)

This likely won't apply to you unless you have a candle app, which would be interesting, to say the least. However, an app is either charged by install or pay-per-click.

- Build On Awareness through Video Views

Considering videos autoplay, this can be an ideal means of fostering awareness in your product and brands. You pay for every 1000 impressions your video garners.

3. Set a Budget

Set a lifetime ad group spend limit. This is not the last time you'll tinker with budgeting in the same ad, but it's the initial step that is required to move forward before you finetune everything.

4. Create an Ad Group

Ad groups can have different budgets and targeting. In addition, since you can have multiple groups, you can have multiple goals within a single campaign. This is helpful when going after different ages, locations, and interests. Some variations of these choices might require a boost in funding or another goal.

5. Set the Target Audience

You'll need to select your target audience based on gender (all, female or male), ages (all, specific age ranges, 21+), locations, languages, devices (all devices, Android mobile or tablet, Apple iPhone or Ipad).

6. Set Ad Placement

You can either choose browse, search, or all. A recommendation is to stick with the 'All' option if at all possible. Browse placements end up in users' home feeds and related pins, while search results work with keywords.

7. Assign Interests and Keywords

Pinterest is a massive place and you're not looking to feature in every interest and keyword. That's crazy and, frankly, very expensive. So instead, when you're selecting interests, find any and all interests relating to candles. You're not going to pick animals or architecture, for example, because your candles don't bark and, no matter how talented you are, they don't design buildings.

With keywords, you're going to practice what I've been preaching in multiple chapters: choose relevant keywords in abundance (25 to be exact) while also utilizing long-tail keywords. You can also include negative keywords to exclude specific search terms which end up triggering your ads, e.g. if you sell dog related candles, you can exclude 'cat'.

Keyword formatting;

- **Broad match:** scented candle

This is when your ad is shown for all close variants of the term as well as synonyms.

- **Phrase match:** "scented candle"

This is when your ad is shown for close variants of your keywords but not for synonyms.

- **Exact match:** [scented candle]

When your ad only shows if a person types in your exact keyword or phrase.

8. Confirm Everything and Schedule

Set the dates for when your ad starts and ends, then set a daily budget for your campaign overall. Consider what daily budgets you gave individual ad groups when you were setting them up.

9. Optimization and Pacing

Set a maximum bid for your Pinterest ads, also known as a CPM rate (cost-per-mille). Minimum bids have to be above $2. You'll also set the pacing of your ad, which is either standard or accelerated.

Standard pacing will align your bid, overall spend and duration of the campaign. On the other hand, accelerated pacing enables faster delivery of your budget and produces more immediate results. Accelerated pacing will likely drain your overall budget rather quickly.

10. Pick Pins You Want to Promote

You can click 'Pick a Pin' to add pins to your desired ad groups in the ad section. Aim for 2-4 images per ad group. For a pin to qualify, the pin must;

- Be saved to your profile
- Not be saved on secret boards
- Have destination URLs
- Feature no third-party content such as videos, gifs or branding.

11. Monitor Performance

This is true with every social media platform, every ad account and any website. If you can monitor analytics, then you should be doing just that, analyzing! Review your clicks, impressions, CTR (click-through rate), eCPM (earned and non-earned cost-per-impression) and eCPC (effective cost-per-click).

Take your time and dive deep into the numbers, stats and graphs. Look for areas where you can improve your ad to get the best reach at the best price.

Types of Pinterest Ads

There are five kinds of Pinterest ads available for you to focus on, use and take advantage of on Pinterest. You've got promoted pins, promoted carousels, prompted video, story pins, and buyable pins. You'll need to compare the ad types, consider your content and goals and decide which ad type suits your ad needs.

Ads are currently set up as 'One-tap' ads. The moment a user taps or clicks on your ad, it takes them to your desired landing page directly and immediately.

Promoted Pin

Promoted pins are showcased in home feeds amongst organic pins and feature a 'Promoted' label on the image letting people know it's an ad. They behave exactly the same way a standard organically found pin would act; the difference is the label. Once reshared, the promoted pin loses the 'Promoted' label.

To promote a pin on Pinterest, it needs to follow the following spec guidelines;

- Campaign objective: Brand awareness
- File type: .PNG or .JPEG
- Ideal aspect ratio: 2:3
- File size: Max 10 MB
- Description copy: Max 500 characters

Promoted Carousel

A promoted carousel is a collection of two to five images presented as a carousel. They also appear amongst organic pins while featuring the 'Promoted' label and three dots indicating multiple viewable images. Each image can have different titles, descriptions, and even landing pages! This is great for promoting various products, with the landing being your product pages on Etsy or your website.

To promote a carousel on Pinterest, it needs to follow the following spec guidelines;

- File type: .PNG or .JPEG
- Ideal aspect ratio: 1:1 or 2:3
- File size: Max 10 MB
- Title copy: Max 100 characters
- Description copy: Max 500 characters

Promoted Video

Similar to a promoted pin, promoted videos are just pins that feature dynamic video content instead of static images. Video ads automatically play on users' feeds and are set to mute unless the sound is added manually. As a result, your video can't rely on audio. It needs to rely instead on visuals to sell a product. Video ads can either be standard or max-width. The difference between the two options is that standard is the same size as regular pins, while max-width spreads across the user's feed.

To promote a video on Pinterest, it needs to follow the following spec guidelines;

- File type: .MPR or .MOV
- Encoding: H264
- Ideal aspect ratio: 1:1, 2:3, 9:16 or 16:9.
- File size: Max 2GB
- Video length: Minimum 4 sec, maximum 15 min
- Description copy: Max 500 characters

Story Pins

Story Pins appear in home feeds with a cover image and a title. Users have the choice to view the stories by tapping on the image and viewing all its pages. You can feature roughly 20 pages of images, text, and links.

Buyable Pins

Buyable Pins allow users to 'shop the look' by finding products within pins and going to their product page. The products are tagged with dots that are displayed when the image is tapped/clicked on. For example, a living room contains multiple types of furniture. You can tag all the furniture and decor items you sell in the image and drive traffic to your product pages on Etsy or your Website.

Pinterest offers a bespoke tagging tool to aid you in the creation of your own Buyable pins. However, if you're working with more extensive campaigns, consider using Olapic or Curalate. Both are Pinterest's Preferred Partners meaning you'll get seamless integration between the platforms.

Tips and Tricks for Pinterest Ads

There are many ways to improve your ads on Pinterest. Here are some tips and tricks I've used over the years that have worked wonders for my presence on Pinterest and my overall sales.

- **Create Beautiful Content**

If you can't produce stunning, aesthetically pleasing images, then you won't survive on Pinterest. This app is packed with beautiful content; content lacking in quality won't survive up against content that has quality in abundance. Focus on vertical images considering 80% of pinners use Pinterest on their mobile devices (Hootsuite, 2019).

- **Lead with a Hook**

The first 30-60 characters of your pin's description matter the most. This is what is seen unless the user chooses to expand and view the full description. So, focus on making this part as engaging as possible. Make sure to include your brand name in the first or second line to boost awareness.

Pro Tip:

> When showcasing your brand visually, be sure to do so in the first few seconds of a video. In images, avoid the lower right corner where it might get covered.

- **Provide Detailed Descriptions**

Quality images matter, but that doesn't mean the words behind the picture matter any less. Therefore, ensure your descriptions or images are detailed and answer any potential questions one might have when they see it themselves.

- **Stick with Lifestyle Themes**

Show your product in action rather than just your product isolated. Obviously, in some cases, this is unavoidable. Still, when consumers can see your product within a lifestyle scene, they can imagine it within their home more or take some inspiration from it. This is especially true in the case of videos.

Pins that show someone interacting with your product or service are 67% more likely to drive online sales lift (Hootsuite, 2019).

Pro Tip:

> The key is to make sure your product is a focal point of the image or video and doesn't get lost in the noise.

- **Add a Text Overlay**

Don't go crazy and turn a beautiful image into an online commercial billboard. However, don't be afraid of adding in some text overlay to entice people further into purchasing your product. For example, when a product is new, tell people it's 'NEW!', overlays with actionable copy see a 6 percent lift in online sales (Hootsuite, 2019).

- **Tell a Story**

When it comes to your visuals, try to tell a story. People are more inclined to watch ads in their entirety if there's a semi-engaging story element attached to the delivery. This type of content can be perfect for your brand story, company news, product launches, showcases, etc.

- **Share 'How-tos'**

Get creative and create some 'How-to' videos or cover images that lead to a blog post where you expand on the how-to. I think video how-tos on

Pinterest are great because you can showcase your product, personality, and brand all in one.

- **Pin for Seasonal Moments**

Don’t leave season moment Pinterest content to the last minute! Instead, plan well in advance to release captivating content that will attract pinners and lure them to click on the link to your store. Christmas, Easter, Back To School, Halloween, Thanksgiving, Diwali the list goes on.

- **Plan for Pin Continuity**

If someone clicks on your pin, it means they’re somewhat interested and want to know more. Therefore, you need to ensure that interested pinners land on a page with helpful and relevant information that can provide the answers that they need. If you can use the same image for continuity, then do it!

- **Use Rich Pins**

The four types of rich pins to better contextualize information for your pins are app, product, article, or recipe. Additionally, including pricing can result in higher online sales.

Key Takeaway

A creative Pinterest is one of the best ways to grow your social standing online. The benefits of this platform are far-reaching, and you can achieve unprecedented growth like no other platform can truly replicate. Pinterest also happens to be a platform filled with people in your likely target market. If you were selling cars, I’d tell you to be less bothered with Pinterest. Thankfully you’re selling candles, and that falls into a decorative category which might as well be how I describe Pinterest.

While some of the numbers might come across as relatively high (30 posts a day, every day), the truth is that it's really a lot easier than it sounds. Once you've spent enough time mastering your approach, achieving something like the 10 minutes of Pinterest a day will be the easiest thing you do all week.

I think the most crucial part about Pinterest is to not get demotivated. It is going to take a fair amount of time to really get any traction on the social media platform. However, once you've thrown yourself into it for a few months, you'll find that things start picking up and your content resonates with your target audience more and more. You can repin old content to show it to your new followers and watch the posts that didn't initially do well all of a sudden thrive. It's a strange place to be, but it's also one of the best places to start marketing your website, Etsy store, brand, and products overalls.

Chapter 7: The Overlooked Power of Email Marketing and Media Outreach

In recent years there's been this strong perception that email marketing is essentially dead. I couldn't disagree more. There is an incredible amount of power to be had in having such a deep connection with your audience. Getting someone to sign up for your newsletters is by no means easy, so when you achieve this crucial step, you're creating another tie to your audience.

Email marketing is by no means easy. It requires a lot of effort but, if done right, the benefits speak for themselves. With effective email marketing, you'll be able to attract and retain customers.

In this chapter, we're going to explore the wild world of email marketing. We're also going to be taking a look beyond that to understand PR (public relations) and media outreach.

Email Marketing

So why does email marketing matter? Let's start with some basic facts about the effectiveness of email marketing.

- 91% of US adults like to receive promotional emails from companies they do business with (MarketingSherpa, 2016).
- Email marketing is more likely to garner sales than social media marketing (OptinMonster, 2019).
- Email marketing has a return on investment (ROI) of $36 for every $1 spent (Constant Contact, 2021).
- According to 80% of professionals, email marketing drives customer acquisition and retention (eMarketer, 2016).
- Marketers who used segmented campaigns noted as much as a 760% increase in revenue (HubSpot, 2021).
- Click-through rates are 100.95% higher in segmented email campaigns than non-segmented campaigns (Mailchimp)

Benefits of Email Marketing

Okay, you know a little bit about why email marketing is essential based on a few stats, but what are the benefits of email marketing? There are so many; where do I even begin!

1.Owning Your Media and Contact Lists

There's a big difference between email and social media marketing. With social media, you don't own anything. You don't own your posts, your follower list, nothing. If Instagram shuts down tomorrow, you've lost everything, and there's no way of getting it back. In that scenario, how many followers are you left with overall? Email marketing isn't like that. When you put the work in and build up an email list, you own that hard work. The only person who can take that away from you is a person who unsubscribes. Additionally, you own the content you produce and send out, a stark difference from many social media platforms.

2. Targeted and Personalized Content

When you send out an email from whichever platform you've chosen to use, you want to ensure its personalized. With automatic email services, you can segment your audience and include code which can personalize the email with their details such as their name. This, in combination with a stellar subject line, quality content, and well-worded text, means you're hitting all the right notes to resonate with your customer base.

Pro Tip:

> Click-through rates are 100.95% higher in segmented email campaigns so make sure you segment your email lists (MailChimp, Unknown).

3. Builds Credibility and Establishes Authority

Email marketing provides a ton of space to create an image of professionalism. But, you'll find that your credibility skyrockets over time, and you will become an authoritative figure. Of course, some won't notice the effort, but many will and that's what matters. To come across as professional it doesn't even require an insane amount of effort. Most email automation platforms have well-designed templates ready for you to customize. Of course, you can take it up a notch with more professionally designed templates, but in the beginning, play around with the templates provided to save time and effort.

4. Improved Brand Recognition

With email marketing, you're reaching out to your customers constantly. As a result, you're showcasing your brand to them consistently, and that's not going to go unnoticed. When you provide quality, valuable content, your audience is going to start to anticipate your email! However, this also means they notice when you stop providing quality-driven content. Make sure you consider the responsibility of email marketing. When Susan from Sacramento is waiting on your email and it doesn't arrive, she might not be too happy with you and this could break trust.

5. Stronger Customer Relationships

By keeping your customers up-to-date on everything that's going on in your business, you're building a relationship. This isn't a relationship you just throw away as sometimes it can be impossible to get back. What's worse, when you stop emailing, services like

Gmail actually rat you out and offer for their users to unsubscribe to your emails. Consistency is key and means stronger customer relationships, remaining relevant and building trust. I cannot emphasize enough how vital these things are for your business.

6. Optimize Your Time and Budget

Maybe I scared you a little back there with all the talk of consistency. I'm not saying spend your entire day sitting at a computer having panic attacks about emails. Be smart about this! There are a ton of email softwares to help you automate your email marketing. One of them is even called Autopilot! The cost in the beginning is relatively low, so there are no excuses.

7. Increased Traffic to Your Website and Online Store

Email marketing is essentially just one big call to action. You load your emails up with links to your store, website, products and social media then create a compelling statement telling your subscriber what to do. This can be an excellent way for customers to connect with you further. But, more importantly, your customers will be more inclined to make their way to spending money on your fabulous candles.

8. Build Excitement

Nobody can deny a customer's love for discounts, exclusives and freebies. So when you've got a well-populated email database, you've also got a network to distribute exclusive offers. This adds value to your emails which encourages people to sign up. Beyond the offers, you can build hype around new products, seasonal products, and limited edition items. Giving your most loyal following exclusive access makes them feel more important and can really influence their spending. You're rewarding their support and loyalty with a few specials or exclusives. In return, you're getting an increase in sales. Win, win, am I right?

9. Immediate Results and Optimization

Your analytics will update quickly and you can see exactly how your email is performing. The power in this short window, between sending out emails and watching the results, means you can pinpoint times when you maybe didn't achieve the results you'd hoped for. With this information, you can dive deeper into reasons why it happened and optimize your emails to try and improve them. Don't be afraid to tiptoe the line that is clickbait.

Pro Tip:

> Make sure you are A/B testing your emails to optimize them. I will go into more detail about this later in the chapter.

10. Reach People Easier

Email marketing is accessible, considering most users open emails on their phones. When you're combining email marketing with the other types of marketing I've gone over in the book already, you're leaving no space for your brand to not be top of mind. There's power in being visible across various high-profile social media platforms and directly in your customers' inboxes.

11. Generate More Leads

With email marketing, you'll quickly find the people that are most interested in what you're offering. Then, you can work to win over holdouts far easier by segmenting your leads and marketing slightly more aggressively to them to produce a sale.

12. Boosts Sales

This should be a given. Email marketing can lead to a boost in sales. This might not be substantial every time you send out an email blast. Still, overall, you'll notice small to more significant sales increases every time an email goes out. 66% of consumers have made a purchase online due to a marketing email (Direct Marketing Association, 2021). All the groundwork you lay with the numerous other benefits I've mentioned will produce results. As long as your content remains relevant, consistent and targeted, you'll find your customers more inclined to make a purchase.

How To Get Started With Email Marketing

Hopefully, now you see the importance of email marketing, and you're ready to try your hand at it yourself! Email marketing isn't as difficult as it may seem. Sure, in the beginning, it's going to be a process of trial and error, but once you've learned from your errors, there's no stopping you. So how do you start?

1.Establish Your Goals

What are you looking to gain from email marketing? Are you looking for sign-ups to build out your list? Hoping to achieve more significant sales? Define your specific goals and work towards achieving them.

2. Building Out Your List

The funny thing about email marketing is that you need your customers' email addresses and you need a fair amount of them. Sadly you can't do much without these all-important email addresses, so be sure to start getting people to sign up!

Here are a few ways to encourage people to sign up:

- Have a pop up on your website with a discount code if they sign up.
- Have a place for people to sign up at the bottom of your website
- Put a link in your social media bio with an incentive to sign up
- Put a link on your thank you cards in your candle packages

3. Content

The average person receives over a hundred emails a day, which honestly sounds like torture. How are you going to stand out? Considering that alarming number, I'd suggest trying to not overdo your content. Less is more, especially considering that everyone's time is limited. You can't be expecting people to read an email that's ten pages long and double-sided. If Ross won't do it to win Rachel back, nobody will do it to buy your candles!

Try to incorporate some video content as 90% of consumers said product videos aided them in decision-making before purchasing a product (Future Learn, 2021).

4. Set Up A Campaign

It's time to set up a campaign, and you'll need to figure out what kind you intend to use. You've got options. Are you sending out a newsletter? Product announcement? Sharing a relevant blog post? Consider what is best for your audience and marketing needs. Additionally, you can create multiple lists so people can sign up for a newsletter but not product launch information, vice versa, or both. This will be more to manage, but it can motivate some to sign up if they know they can receive the part of your email marketing that they actually want to be a part of.

5. Schedule Your Emails

Having a set schedule of when you intend to post is great for planning ahead. However, it's also good for customers as they start looking forward to your emails. Another benefit of this structured model is utilizing random email blasts for product announcements, special offers, etc. This will surprise your audience, who were otherwise not expecting an email. This can build excitement.

Pro Tip:

> Make sure you analyze your analytics to discover what time is best for your audience. If you nail this, you can expect higher open and click through rates (CTR)!

6. Track Results

Always track the results of each and every email you send. You need to know how many people are opening your emails, how many people are traveling to the links you've provided (your CTR), how many are unsubscribing, and more. Understanding these metrics means you can find out what is and isn't working and change your email strategy accordingly.

Best Email Automation Services

There are many services available to make your life easier and your email marketing more manageable. We're going to explore a few of those services. I highly recommend purchasing an email marketing software as this can save you a huge amount of time, whilst keeping you organized.

ActiveCampaign

Starts at $9/ month

If you're a small business, then ActiveCampaign is probably the best service for you.

ActiveCampaign offers so many customer experience automation (CXA) tools you can use to reach your customers more effectively. For example, it offers email, SMS, site messaging, and Customer Relations Management (CRM) functionality. The whole concept of ActiveCampaign is to be a visual canvas where you can create functional, automated marketing sequences across a wide array of channels.

ActiveCampaign offers one of the best A/B split tests of any email automation service, most of which don't even offer it at all. A/B split test means you can test anything from the subject lines to the number of touchpoints, delays between emails, and so much more. This is a valuable tool to ensure your marketing is optimized.

Notable Features Include:

- 125+ Email templates
- 500+ Automation recipes
- 800+ Integrations
- Landing pages
- SMS messaging
- Custom reporting
- Web personalization
- CRM (Customer Relationship Management)
- Split actions and A/B Testing
- Predictive content
- Predictive sending
- Goal tracking and attribution

Drip

Starts at $19/ month

If you're a small-medium e-commerce business, then Drip is probably the best service for you.

Drip, as a platform, focuses heavily on integration with the mainstream e-commerce platforms like Shopify, WooCommerce, and Magento, as well as far smaller platforms. With Drip, you can interact with your customers across various channels, such as SMS, social media, email, and more. Overall, Drip has positioned itself as the product to aid businesses in growing e-commerce stores.

Notable Features Include:

- Visual automation
- Email and SMS marketing
- Dynamic e-commerce content blocks
- Discount codes
- e-commerce Segmentation
- Retargeting
- e-commerce store integrations
- Reporting dashboards
- Split testing sequences

AutoPilot

Starts at $49/month for 2,000 contacts

AutoPilot as a platform has tried to make email marketing as straightforward and collaborative as possible. They've achieved this through the use of an unconventional method of annotation using emojis. Anyone on a team can annotate the automation with emojis, stickers, and explanations to facilitate a more streamlined automation creation process. AutoPilot also allows for trigger actions. If you learn to fully understand this process, you're going to have more time on your hands than you know what to do with!

ConvertKit

Starts at $9/month for 300 subscribers

This is the barebones alternative for people looking for something straightforward. There are no email templates as the platform promotes the concept of text-based emails over heavily designed emails. I think that if this works for you, great. However, there is always room for email newsletters to have some imagery to add a bit of character and reference. You want people to know what you actually make and how your products look.

Recommendation

My recommendation is to use ActiveCampaign or Drip. I've tried both and have found they're both well-equipped platforms to facilitate growth. I use ActiveCampaign at the moment and have found great success in using the service. It's important to note that not everyone will have the same experience. While I don't use ConvertKit, that doesn't mean it's not for you! My word is not law, and you need to determine what platform works best for you and your business by doing your own research.

I've spoken so much about email services that I'd recommend, but there are two I want to highlight as services to avoid. In my experience, Hubspot and Mailchimp are not services you want to use for email marketing automation. Why? They're so expensive, and the more you grow, the worse the fee becomes. This is such a deterrent for growth and damaging to your bottom line, so it makes more sense to find a service that does the job as effectively but at a far better price. Furthermore, in terms of Mailchimp, the platform has become so convoluted that understanding it will take a fair amount of time, defeating the purpose of making life easier. Additionally, you don't actually own your contacts which defeats the whole purpose of setting an email list up!

What Factors Should Influence Your Decision?

- Cost: You want an automation service that's worth the money it's charging every month. Email marketing services can get expensive, and they can do so very quickly. So make sure you consider the scaling costs before you choose a software.

- UX (User Experience): Is the software easy to use? I've said it already, but MailChimp is a disaster when it comes to UX. Maybe not ten years ago, but they've overdone their interface to the point where it's a nightmare. As a result of a terrible interface (they are also overpriced), I'll never consider using them again.

- Deliverability: You need to make sure the service that you choose is up to the task and delivers your emails quickly. You want to invest your time, energy, and money into a service that can

1. Flag clients for review if their emails keep bouncing.
2. Remove email addresses associated with problematic clients
3. Monitor your blacklists
4. Manage IP address reputation

- Features: Every email automation service offers standard features and then pro features. Explore all the additional features to see if anything can be helpful to your marketing needs, especially as you start to scale your business. However, be careful not to be lured in by excessive additional features. Some less than stellar platforms have extra features that really provide a smoke and mirror effect, with features that are not actually useful for a product business.
- CRM (Customer Relationship Management): You can choose a separate CRM. However, I do not advise this until you are a multimillion dollar business, it makes no sense to over complicate your business for now. A CRM system is essentially a big database to store all your data, this can help with customer support and complaints. However, most email services have a small CRM built in which is perfectly fine when you are first starting

out. An integrated CRM triggers emails to the right people and creates a sales channel with your customers.

- Reporting: What good is email marketing if you can't monitor how it's going? You need complete transparency to see where you're succeeding and failing in order to implement changes and optimize your approach. Look for a service that offers comprehensive and easy-to-understand reporting so you can constantly improve and make more sales!

- Support and training: Customer support can be a pain, but when you need it, it's a godsend. Don't ignore this aspect of the platform you choose. You don't want to end up in a position where you can't find anyone to help you solve a time sensitive problem.

While not as essential in my eyes, training can be something to look out for in a platform. Learning how to utilize the service can be highly informative and can actually improve your sales immensely.

- Security: You're dealing with a lot of sensitive information. You want to ensure your chosen email service is an online impenetrable fortress of data that can't be accessed by anyone but you! The last thing you want to happen is the information of thousands of subscribers is hacked, accessed, or stolen.

How To Optimize Your Email Content

It's one thing to send emails with an attitude of producing high-quality, valuable content, but how do you optimize your emails to help them reach their fullest potential?

For starters, you need to get familiar with improving deliverability by monitoring metrics! These are the metrics you're going to become very close with as you become an email marketing aficionado;

Open Rate

The open rate represents how many emails were actually opened out of the last batch of emails you sent. If these numbers are low, there are a variety of things you can change to try and improve it. You should target and improve your subject line, sender name, and preheader text! You need to try and make your subject line more catchy, so it peaks your subscribers' interests enough for them to open the email.

Pro Tip:

> Try and change one thing at a time so if your open rate does improve you know what caused it. If you changed 5 parts of your email, how do you know which part was actually the catalyst for change?

Click-Through Rate

All those wonderful links you've included, are they actually being opened? Now you'll know, thanks to the click-through rate! You can use this metric to improve content delivery. If your CTR is low, try and do some A/B testing, focus on the headings, call to action and text order.

Pro Tip:

> Keep your emails short, no one will click a link 3 pages in, it's just not realistic, everyone has a short attention span.

Bounce Rate

Sometimes, people just mess up their email addresses and sometimes your email is too spammy. Usually if you are manually capturing emails through forms or sometimes online too. There are two types of bounce rates; soft and hard bounce rates.

A soft bounce rate is when an email can't be received due to a full inbox. This can be remedied eventually on the customer's end, meaning the email will be received when they stop hoarding emails.

A hard bounce, on the other hand, is when the email address is invalid. You need to keep an eye on this and remove such email addresses immediately. Having a low bounce rate improves your sender reputation and reduces the likelihood of your emails going into people's spam.

Unsubscribe Rate

People come and go like seasons which is an indirect quote from the 2006 smash hit ‘Fergalicious’ (god, I feel old). She was right, of course, and this applies to email marketing too! People will often subscribe under the guise of getting a special offer or freebie, only to leave once they’ve received it. Sometimes it’s about the quality of the content they’re receiving. Regardless, you want to try and keep your unsubscribe rate under 0.5% at all times! If your unsubscribe rate is higher, a larger percentage of your emails will be sent to people's spam inbox, reducing your customer reach.

Conversion Rate

The all-important conversion rate tells you how many people actually buy from your site through a particular email. It answers the question of how many emails are actually converting into sales and revenue earned?

Overall, there are a ton of rates, but I rate you’ve got it! To optimize your content to improve your rates and results you can utilize A/B testing to try variations of your content. Remember, you’ll need to test it in isolation, one thing at a time, and change things like headings, CTAs, copy, and photos!

How To Get The Most Out Of Your Emails

There are many ways in which you can get the most out of each and every email you send out to your adoring fans.

- **Pay special attention to your subject line and opening line**

First impressions are so important as they set the tone for everything. When you see a person and you instantly don't like them, it's difficult, if not impossible, for them to change that opinion. The same goes for email subject lines and opening lines. If your subscribers find your subject line is filled with spammy language, they'll avoid the email and move on. You won't even get the chance to change their minds because they won't even see what you have to say or show. Also, don't make the subject line too long. Your audience is not going to see it all as email platforms eventually cut it off. Then you've just got an incomplete thought as your subject line. Finally, the opening line is previewed before even going into the email, and a bad opening line isn't going to seal any deals.

Pro Tip:

> Don't be afraid to create catchy, click bait email subject lines. The sole aim of a subject line is to get someone to open your email.

- **Speak conversationally**

Readability is vital when it comes to email marketing as you are trying to connect with your customers. Don't use massive words that won't resonate with your audience or, worse, cause them to pick up a dictionary. Instead, speak like you're talking to a friend, but know the boundaries, and sell them on your brand. Again, this is just advice, this is extremely dependent on your brand message and tone of voice.

- **Impart a sense of urgency**

Manufacture a sense of urgency in what you're offering. For example, saying things like 'limited stock' or 'only valid for 24 hours' informs people that they need to act now unless they want to end up disappointed.

- **Make sure you personalize**

Personalize the interactions with your customers as much as possible. You can use tools like Optimail and Marketo to truly learn how your customer has and does interact with your business. This can make it easy to include these groups of people in more targeted emails regarding things they frequently look at, purchase, interact with, and more.

Pro Tip:

> Use the email software tools to personalize each email. For example, you can add your customer's name into the subject line,

address it to them personally and include any other personal information you have on them in a few simple clicks!

- **Segment your users**

Segmenting your users can yield more positive results in your email marketing approach. Try and segment your audience into categories of what they viewed the most, what they interact with the most, geography, age, or anything that sets them apart. Then you can target that need and elicit a sale out of them through specific discounts and offers.

- **Include a strong CTA (Call To Action)**

An email you send out is never the end of the conversation. You need to include a CTA telling your customers what to do with this email they've just received. Suppose you're sending out emails that don't lead to other places like a blog post, product page, special offer, free digital offering, or something of that nature. In that case, you're wasting your time and leaving money on the table.

- **Use rich-text**

Don't be afraid of incorporating various rich-text into your email to highlight key information, e.g. **Bold,** *italics*, ALL CAPS, underlining, and different size fonts.

This acts as a stimulant to the brain and keeps people more engaged when you use unpredictable, rich text. Who doesn't love a little bit of a surprise in their emails?

- **Optimize for all devices**

Most people use their phones, but some still use computers, and others use tablets. So you're never catering to just one device. As a result, you need to ensure your emails look great on all devices.

Pro Tip:

> On most email software you can preview calibration on different devices to make sure that your emails look good on all the most popular phones, tablets and computers.

- **Put yourself in their shoes**

There are things that you know for a fact you'd tear apart if you were on the receiving end of an email blast. You want to treat your emails as harshly as you do others. When you send out a test version of your newsletter, you'll need to look at the email objectively. Search for errors in grammar and spelling, check the links work, ensure pictures load properly and are easy to view, etc. Essentially make sure there are ZERO errors in what is meant to be a very professional means of communication.

Pro Tip:

> ALWAYS test your emails before you send them out to customers, the last thing you want is to send the most amazing email and then the link is broken.

- **Offer a Variety Of Sharable Links**

Make it easy for your customers to do the work of reaching new audiences for you! Provide ample shareable links, promote the concept of sharing the email with their friends, family, followers, whomever, and watch their efforts translate into sign-ups and sales.

- **Provide an Unsubscribe Button**

Imagine being in an escape room with no escape? Not a fun experience. Some customers sign up for an email blast before realizing that maybe it was a mistake, or they lose interest, don't like what you have to say, or whatever the case might be, and that's fine. It's not super awesome, but it's okay. You are not a hostage keeper. You need to let them GO! Including an unsubscribe link is non-negotiable and is actually illegal in many countries (e.g. the UK)! Make it easy to find, easy to achieve and, if you can, ask them why they're leaving. Maybe you can learn from their departure and can optimize your email strategy more going forward.

- **Evaluate your sender name**

When your email lands in an inbox, what is the sender's name? Make it crystal clear that it's your brand, or people might just avoid reading the email altogether. If you've got subcultures in the form of segmented audiences for things like 'Candle of the Month Club,' then make sure your sender name declares that explicitly.

Media/PR outreach

We've spent so much time talking about social media and email marketing which are places where you're in control. It's time to consider another avenue of marketing that offers far less control but can produce incredible results, media/PR outreach.

PR outreach is pretty straightforward. You pitch your brand, product and, in some cases, yourself to journalists, bloggers, influencers, and anyone else with a bit of reach in the hopes of getting exposure. The exposure can come in the form of brand mentions, press coverage, and anything that brings awareness to you and what you have to offer.

Ideally, you're going to want to build a relationship with the journalists, influencers, and whoever you intend to elicit help from, as going in without any prior relationship can result in a frosty reception and more often than not, no response at all. I'm not suggesting you go on a wild night out with them and ask for a shoutout while downing your seventh Cosmo. If that's your tactic, then I can't stop you. Still, I was thinking more along the lines of some light professional conversation, a follow on social media, some comments on their work - obviously positive. Nobody wants to work with a person who degrades their work. A foundational relationship can be the thing that gets you in the door, while a lack of one can have that same door promptly shut on your face.

The benefit of press outreach means you're gaining access to an audience that's likely large and has probably never heard of you. For customers, hearing about your business from a trusted source that they've deemed credible can impart that credibility onto your products.

Tips to Improve Your Press Outreach

Here are a few helpful tips for improving your press outreach. So before you start working the phones, emails, and charm, consider some of these pieces of advice first!

- **Know Who You're Targeting**

When approaching a journalist, blogger, or anyone in the press, you want to know who they are before selling yourself and your brand. Another reason why this matters is, what good is pitching your candle business to Joe Racetrack, who writes all about cars? I'm not sure I need to clarify this, but there's no situation where the two would be used simultaneously. Nobody's lighting up candles while competing in Formula One. You need to know who this person is, what they've written, and if they're worth reaching out to in the first place.

- **Build a Specific Media List**

You need to be prepared. Creating a specific media list means you;

1. Define the content you're pitching
2. Develop unique angles
3. Decide the timing
4. Search by publication and writer.

Once A-D has been completed, then you reach out. Reaching out before you've defined the content or developed unique angles means you're winging it. Nobody enjoys their time being wasted, especially in the fast-paced business that is journalism. Unique angles make your content more interesting to a broader array of journalists. This is great because if Larry from Arts and Crafts magazine rejects you, at least you've got the prospects of Sarah from Lifestyle magazine saying yes! Timing matters if the content you're hoping to get out there is time-sensitive. Long lead publications work 3-6 months in advance. At the same time, online and daily newspapers, tv and local radio have significantly shorter turnaround times.

Pro Tip:

You need to plan your content based on lead times, for example, you need to be reaching out latest in June/July if you want your candle featured for Halloween in October in print.

- **Search by Publication and Writer**

Start searching for publications closely associated with what you're offering. As you start finding these publications look for the writers in your niche or anyone working in the niche closest to yours. These are the people you want to get a hold of. You might often find that the writers for some of these publications also work with similar publications or ones close enough to your niche. This means you might be able to get into multiple places at once.

- **Focus on Correct Designations**

Some outlets have various designations for journalists and writers. Always pitch to reporters, staff writers, or editorial assistants. Never pitch to an editor-in-chief. They have no business in content creation and are focused on selecting content and creating the overall publication.

- **Write an Attention-Grabbing Subject Line**

Just like with email marketing, you've got to hook your target audience and sell them on your brand, your product, and you! '57% of journalists receive between 50 and 500 pitches per week' (Dragilev, 2021). This horrifying statistic means you need to find a way to stand out without being spammy.

- **Develop Your Relevant Story**

In 200-300 words, pitch your relevant story and consider potential headlines, the key message you're conveying, and the newsworthy elements of the content. Use bullet lists to make it clear what the intention and goals are for the content. If you're offering an exclusive, make it known! Also, if it's an exclusive, potentially plan it ahead of the actual launch.

- **Prove Your Contents Value**

Journalists want content that's credible, newsworthy, and relevant. If you can't correctly identify if your content meets these standards, it probably isn't. For credibility, you must use data to back up any claims made.

Getting Into Magazines

Magazines are perfect places to get into for reaching your target audience. Why? There are so many homemakers, decor, and lifestyle magazines. These are speaking predominantly to women. They can effectively sell your product by showcasing it as a decorative item whilst having practical use.

Most magazines actually follow a similar formula when deciding on their editorial calendar. Andrea from Creative Live actually pinpointed this excellently (Creativelive.com, 2014);

January: Wellness, weight loss, resolutions

February: Valentine's Day gifts, travel

March: Springtime fashion, products, and gardening

April: Earth Day, eco-products, tax tips

May: Mother’s Day, Memorial Day, graduation

June: Father’s Day, graduation, summer style

July: Summer entertaining, barbecues, Fourth of July, weddings

August: Back to school

September: Cool weather fashion

October: Halloween, breast cancer awareness

November: Thanksgiving, recipes, holiday gifts

December: Holiday gifts, parties

There is prime real estate for some exciting pieces on candles in various months. For example, in February where candles can be used for romantic Valentine's dates. Earth Day, where candles can be used at night instead of electricity. May, where a candle can be a part of mom’s special Mother’s Day gift. July when candles can be a fantastic aesthetic feature of weddings. October, where candles can feature in creepy pumpkin carvings. November, when candles can be a part of a Thanksgiving decorative spread. December, where it’s Christmas, and I don’t even need to explain myself.

Consider how your chosen publications go about product roundups. Do they run monthly guides?

Holiday roundups? Annual roundups? These might be questions you need to ask the magazine if it's not explicitly clear. One thing you need to be aware of is preparedness. Publications won't leave things up to the last minute. Instead, they will plan ahead in detail, so make a move quickly if you've got ideas.

When pitching your story, make sure it's engaging, relatable, and fit for the type of publication you're aiming to get featured in. Some great story templates that you can tailor your content to include; Gift Stories, Timing Stories and Problem Solving Stories. For example, a gift story could be something like; 'Best Candles for your Mom this Mother's Day!' A timing story could be 'Best Candles to make Halloween Pumpkins Glow' With problem-solving stories you want to ask and answer a question; 'Power Out? It's Time To Stock Up on Candles!'

Once you've been featured, use it as a launchpad and generate more buzz surrounding your product! Don't let this accomplishment wither away into nothingness. Feature it on your blog, let your audience know about it on social media, and email it out in your newsletter.

Pro Tip:

> If you're not feeling up to the task of doing everything yourself, you can hire professionals to do it all for you! There are a ton of agencies that offer PR services to get you and your brand the attention it deserves.

Launch Grow Joy Media Leads is an excellent example of a PR company that connects you with thousands of magazines, editors, online influencers, and more! It's not a cheap option considering it starts at $125 a month, but it's well worth the consideration. Other notable services include the likes of HARO.

Get in the Local Press

Don't look down on local press as it's just as important because, as the saying goes, 'all press is good press.' When it comes to local press, you've got options; local radio stations, newspapers, consumer magazines, news broadcasts, talk shows, events, etc. Find any avenue willing to let you tell your story, and you'll find that results in your area spike. No matter where it comes from, a sale is a sale, so don't turn your back on the local press.

Key Takeaways

No one told you email marketing would be this way. Well, I just did, and it's not something to be afraid of! This is a lucrative marketing opportunity that can produce better results than some of the other social media options available! Imagine how effective your marketing apparatus will be when you're utilizing all the major social media platforms, email marketing, and even public relations! Are you even going to have enough candles to fulfill all the orders? We haven't even broken into the world of wholesale yet, and I'm already worried you're going to be sold out before then!

In my eyes, this is the biggest trial and error method of social marketing to get right. However, once you manage to fully understand what you're doing and how to do it, this will create a lot of opportunities for sales. Furthermore, it will foster much more profound relationships with your clients.

Chapter 8: Selling Your Product Face-to-face

I've been talking so much about utilizing online selling. However, I want to clarify that there is still room for face-to-face interactions. There's no need to abandon physical selling altogether. You're not doing anyone any favors by neglecting this side of your business. You need to get out there, go to farmers markets, market yourself and your brand/product in person to people that you meet.

I'm going to break it all down for you so that you can sell your candles like there's no tomorrow!

How To Sell at Local Farmers Markets

Farmers markets are havens for locally crafted goods, and you NEED to recognize the potential these venues hold for your bottom line. Of course, not every market will be a success, but finding that needle in a haystack can really turn things around and help boost sales.

There's so much to think about when it comes to farmers markets, starting with the basics of setting up.

Setting Up

You need to take pride in your setup. Just because you're at a farmers market doesn't mean your make-shift storefront needs to look like a pigpen. There are a few things you're going to need to make your store even remotely worth the customer's time.

Before I let you in on the things you need, I want to talk about tables. The likeness is that a table will be provided to you by the venue. For example, some farmers markets have built-in stalls, and others offer tables. Don't get caught out, make sure you ask the venue about tables, as you may need to plan for it in advance.

Here are some of the items you're going to need to bring with you to the farmers market to complete your stall.

1.Table Cloth

I'm going to give you a fair warning, the tables you will likely find available at a farmers market aren't glamorous. You know that farm aesthetic that looks so charming on Pinterest? That's not what you're getting here. You're getting a table that needs to be covered up. Don't go overboard with the table cloth. Be a little plain and boring with a white or black cloth to allow your products to not get lost in patterns and bombastic colors.

Another thing you want to do is get a cloth for the back wall, so you don't have a background of cars, other stalls, or worse, people shoving their faces with food. Any distractions should try to be circumvented.

2. Signage and Marketing Materials

Your candle store isn't 'No Name's Candles', flaunt your brand identity and let people know who you are and what you're selling. My advice is to invest in some banners, posters, and any other marketing material that can announce your presence to people as they walk past. Visually, your store will look great, assuming you don't treat it as Times Square and throw every advertisement under the sun at it. Additionally, you'll have some stellar content for social media, which is always a win!

3. Basic Supplies and Necessities

You're going to need some basic setup supplies to neaten up your stall. Consider carrying with you at all times the following; scissors, cable ties and tape.

Another thing you should probably bring is a coffee flask for a hot drink as the early mornings can be rather nippy. In my experience, they've been bitterly cold and the coffee was the only thing keeping me from lighting all my products and basking in the heat.

Finally, some food or snacks. Snickers said it best; 'you're not you when you're hungry.' Of course, there will be food available at the market. Still, it can be challenging to leave your stall unattended unless you've got a friend or colleague with you. Additionally, it can become quite costly if you're purchasing food every weekend when you are there to make money, not spend it.

4. Business Cards

Something that may never die is the business card. A great reminder for customers about your business days later when they stumble upon it in their wallets. Business cards are great for customers to follow up, ask more questions and most importantly place more orders. After all, market goers see hundreds of stalls and may not remember your business name, a card eliminates this issue.

5. Displays

If you thought a table cloth was all you needed to display your candles, I have bad news. You spent hours making candle after candle; why would you throw them on a table and call it a day? Respect your hard work and your product, and invest in displays to elevate the best candles of the bunch. When you're fighting for attention from the people passing by, a display makes it more evident that they should look at your products as it will catch their eye more easily.

Your display should be intuitive, so try to work with different heights and elevate various products in progressions around the table.

6. Payment Options

Let's be realistic; cash transactions aren't as popular as they used to be. Everyone uses a card these days, and not having a card reader to process your payments will result in more lost sales than you'd care to admit. I've made this mistake only once, and let me tell you, I'll never make it again!

On the other hand, you still need to provide the cash transaction as an option. This means having change ready in case it's needed.

There are also other options available like QR codes which have become more prevalent in the last few years. Giving your customers options provides convenience that makes shopping at your stall easy.

7. Chair

Farmers markets are long days, they can take up the whole morning or evening. There will be times when it's slow, and you'll find yourself with less to do, so having a chair is great for resting your feet. Standing the entire time isn't necessary, and with a chair, your feet won't cry out in pain.

8. Shopping Bags

If you want to irritate your customers, sell them a bunch of candles without anything to carry them in. Make sure you have bags so this doesn't happen! You can use plain bags or go that extra mile and have branded bags; it doesn't matter either way. As long as you have something, that's good enough. Obviously, branded bags are more beneficial for brand awareness. Still, they can cost more and eat into your profits, so this is something you'll need to consider.

Pro Tip:

> Why not stamp plain carrier bags with your logo, this is a cheap alternative to getting branded bags made. This is only an option for some makers, as this may not match your brand aesthetic.

Attracting Customers

You're not the only stall at the farmers market and you may not even be the only candle stall, so you need to fight for business amongst the fields of options. I don't mean you need to be underhanded or aggressive with your neighbors. I mean, be competent in how you market your stall to passersby. This is a farmers market at the end of the day. There's no need to make enemies with the stalls around you.

1.Clear Signage

Aren't we all just looking for a sign? Well, even if we aren't, yours needs to be found easily. Make sure your business name is big and bold, so people don't have to squint to read it. Try to make your signage more prominent than your neighbors by elevating it using the poles and straps of your stall structure.

2. Make Sure It's Clear Who You Are and What You're Selling

Don't leave room for mystery. You're a candle business, not the sequel to Gone Girl. Nobody should be guessing what your business is or trying to figure out who you are. Clear signage only works when you have identified your business's name, logo, brand identity, and everything else that goes into making it clear that you sell candles. You can either achieve this by having it in your business name or noting it on the sign under your business name.

For example;

- Amy Dune's Amazing Candles or
- Dune Creatives - One Stop Candle Shop

3. Have An Amazing Product and Show it Off

Make sure that you're bringing a quality product to the farmers market to sell something you know is worth buying. You're in a haven for artsy, craftsy kinds of products, you have competition all around and your product needs to be shown to be superior. So light a few candles (if allowed), show off that flame, let the smell circulate and lure people in. Show off your hard work and let your candles sell themselves by playing to the senses.

4. Take Pride In Your Stall Setup

It's important to never allow your stall to become untidy. People will grab your products, move things out of line, or mess up your display, and you need to be there to constantly fix it back up. If you've got candles lit, don't let them get too low as this is unattractive, and let's be honest, humans are vain and may be put off by this.

5. Straightforward Pricing

Pricing is so vital when selling at a farmers market. You've got to know where to price your products to make them competitive while still making a profit. Try and cater to all price ranges from the dirt cheap to the high roller (relative to a candle and your branding, of course). You need to appeal to all types of buyers, for example, have $5 wax melts and then $30 candles. Different buyers have different definitions of what they're willing to spend; always keep that in mind when pricing your candles.

Never leave a product without a price attached to it. The moment a customer doesn't know the price, they will potentially just walk away altogether instead of asking. Sometimes people don't like asking in case it is more than they are willing to spend.

Additionally, you'll want to embrace specials. Buy three, get one free, or 20% off, or whatever else you can come up with. People love a deal and sometimes buy things purely based on significant savings, even if the purchase doesn't make sense. Another thing you can experiment with is bundle deals to help sell more stock and, in turn, make more money.

6. Friendly Attitude

It's the 2020s, and people really aren't interested in dealing with rudeness anymore. Word travels far too fast these days. Allowing a poor attitude to ripple into the online world is a recipe for disaster. Smile, be friendly, make small talk, do all the things to make your customers feel invited. A great attitude will shine far brighter than any candle could ever, and that's what could be the determining factor in making a sale.

7. If Possible, Create a Queue

What kind of response does a queue evoke? Mystery. This is by no means a really easy method to achieve, but that doesn't mean it's impossible. Having a queue means you're going to have other people wanting to get in on the action to find out what's so interesting about your stall and your products. People who've waited in line are also more likely to buy something purely because they don't want to have just wasted time in line for nothing. Manipulative marketing at its finest.

8. Get Creative

There's no real right or wrong answer to what 'get creative' means. I'd suggest doing some research and looking at ways to really make your stall stand out. For example, tailoring your stall to the season or holiday time like Christmas or Halloween. It's your stall, and you control what falls under the mandate of getting creative. Still, the main point is a concerted attempt at being unique and offering a visual experience that sucks customers in.

Best Practices for Selling at a Farmers Market

1.Know What You're Talking About

If the people viewing your products have questions, you need to be equipped with all the answers. A knowledgeable salesperson is incredibly beneficial. It provides additional information to the client while creating a sense of confidence in both your product and brand.

2. Look Busy

There will always be a moment during your time at the farmers market where there's a decline in activity. Regardless, you need to always make yourself look busy. Maybe bring some stuff from home to demonstrate something to do with candle-making. You'll add a sense of connection between you and your product and pique people's interest in what you're up to.

3. Ditch the Phone

Be present at all times. Your phone isn't going anywhere, so leave it somewhere safe and accessible so that if you need it, it's there. Otherwise, leave it. Thankfully it's only a day of working, so you won't miss much.

4. Confidence is Key

Be confident in your brand and product and project that onto everyone you come into contact with while selling at the farmers market. You don't want to look unsure of anything. This can lead to a weary customer uncertain if your product is worth parting money over.

5. Take More Stock Than You Might Need Incase

It's better to have and not need than to need and not have. So always take as much as you can to the farmers market, so you're able to stock up during the day if needed. It really doesn't matter if you don't end up needing the extras; it's about having them in case.

Pro Tip:

> People are attracted to full stalls, think about it, have you ever walked past a cake stall where only the scraps are left? I have and I tell you, I walked straight past to the other cake stand. So make sure you are topping up your table wherever needed.

6. Practice Your Setup Ahead of Time

You'll benefit from practicing how you plan to set up so you can be aware of how much time you'll need on the day. Then, you can determine a system to maximize your efficiency. As time goes on and you get more markets under your belt, you'll have mastered your set-up by improving it slowly with more knowledge from every market you work at.

Another benefit of practicing your setup ahead of time is that you can play around with different styles, layouts, products, decor, and other things to make your stall look the best it can be.

7. Arrive Early

You don't want people to start arriving while you're still setting up your stall! That's a nightmare scenario. You'll begin rushing and cutting corners to open up properly and, in doing so, miss crucial steps to making your stall as perfect as possible. Once you lose the time, it's impossible to get it back, and it could result in a lack of sales.

Tips

You can do so many cool things to make your stall the best at the farmers market. Here are just a few tips I implemented and found really worked for my stall.

1.Giveaways always get people signing up to your newsletter

Grow your emailing list with ease by offering a giveaway that requires them to sign up for your newsletter. You'll have a relatively low overhead for the prize but benefit significantly from the email sign-ups, which can help you later on with marketing.

2. Provide samples of other products you might sell

If you have other products where a sample is possible, offer it. Gaining interest in any product at your stall opens the door for all your products.

3. Find what makes you different and advertise that

All businesses have something that makes them unique in some way, shape, or form. First, you need to identify what your it-factor is and make it a part of your identity. Then, showcase it and let people see you're not just any old candle maker!

4. Network

You're surrounded by like-minded people. Therefore, you should utilize every aspect of a farmers market to benefit your business. You could gain valuable insight into other people's practices and maybe learn something that could work for you, and vice versa. You never know who's in attendance at a farmers market, so treat everyone like they might open the door for you and your business.

5. Insurance!

Bad stuff can happen at any moment. I don't want to sound pessimistic, but it's true, anything can happen and you need to be prepared. First, check to make sure your insurance covers farmers markets in case, heaven forbid, something was to happen to your precious stock. If your current insurance doesn't cover farmers markets, purchase extra coverage to protect your bottom line in case of an unfortunate event.

6. Protecting Your Products From the Elements

Candles react differently to different weather conditions. Therefore, you need to be prepared for all of the possible scenarios to ensure you don't lose valuable products because of a bit of heat, rain, or wind. If it's hot, make sure you've got a cover/tarp in combination with a fan to keep your candles cool. This way, they have a far less likely chance of melting. If it's cold and windy, make sure you provide ample shelter to ensure nothing falls and breaks.

How Much Is a Farmers Market Going to Cost You?

There's no real way to quantify an average amount of money for a farmers market because they heavily vary based on;

- Location
- Popularity
- Average Crowd Size
- Days (i.e., markets during festive seasons might be more expensive than off-season)
- Infrastructure and Amenities
- Attractions

I once sold my candles at a farmers market that cost me roughly $50. Still, I paid $900 for a stall at a different, far more popular, farmers market in a great area. These two numbers are so wildly different that putting forth an average is near impossible.

It's essential to take the price into consideration and weigh it against all these factors. In doing so, you'll determine if it's a reasonable price or if it means you might be spending more than you'll end up making. Just because it costs more doesn't mean it's immediately worth it. A higher price tag doesn't necessarily mean you'll be seeing insane sales.

Pro Tip:

> Go and explore all the farmers markets in your area and make real-time evaluations of the crowd size, composition, location, other vendors, and attractions. Then, use this information to determine if you can make the specific farmers market work for you and your business.

Additionally, try to determine how many candles you'll need to sell in order to make it worth doing and consider if that number is an achievable figure.

Deciding if the Farmers Market Is Actually Worth Your Time

Eventually, you're going to have to assess if a farmers market is the best route for you and your business. Ask yourself the question; is this audience the right audience for my product? Have I done all I can to sell my product effectively? Am I seeing results? Am I spending more doing the farmers market than I'm making?

My advice is to try many different markets out, consider planning out a way to go to a different market every weekend. Then once you know the best venues, repeat a pattern of visiting the popular ones. This way, you never become stagnant in just one market where the same people attend every week.

Selling Locally

Why stop at just selling at farmer's markets? There's a whole big world out there, and I think you should ignore that for a second and think about selling locally.

Have you got a car? Yes? Great! Maybe you can offer free delivery within a specific radius. However, be sure to clarify that radius ahead of time before you disappoint someone out of reach. You don't want to find yourself in the hole for excessive gas prices because of a slip-up with the delivery radius.

If you don't have a car, there are other ways to offer free delivery. For example, services like Uber will do package deliveries for a fee that can sometimes be partially or wholly absorbed into the product's overall price. This way, you're not losing any money on the delivery method at all but still offering it as a free service.

So how do you let the locals know that you're offering a product with free delivery?

Flyers

Flyers remain a really effective marketing tool even as the world dives headfirst into a more technologically driven age. There's no better way to promote your business locally than to utilize flyers to make people aware of your company, product and how to purchase what you're selling.

What Should Your Flyer Look Like and What Needs To Be Included

To have a flyer that sells people on your brand and product, you need to consider the following;

1.Clarity

Make sure your brand name, the product you're selling, contact information, directions to get the deal and all information is presented in a way that makes sense. You need to thoroughly explain why the flyer exists, to begin with, all while being concise.

2. Professional Photos

What is the point of a flyer if your images aren't professional? You'll make a terrible impression and will have wasted lots of money on flyers that see a trash can far sooner than they cause anyone to make a purchase. So my recommendation is to stick with a minimum of 300 DPI on every image printed and make sure you put your best foot forward by choosing your images carefully.

3. Readable font (brand font or a font in-line with brand font)

You don't want to go below 10 points for the flyer's body, as that's when things become challenging to read. Beyond size, make sure you pick fonts in line with your brand that are easy to read and consistent. This is more important for your headlines as that is what catches most attention.

4. Specials or deals made clear

Make sure the deal you're promoting is explained using concise language while remaining easy to understand. Keep it simple and don't make the process of enjoying the special offer difficult.

5. Splashes of color

Don't be afraid to be bold with your color choices. More daring color choices help to draw attention to your flyers, even from a distance.

Pro Tip:

> Make sure these colors are in line with your brand as it may be confusing if not!

Where Should These Flyers Be Going?

There is no shortage of options for where to go to distribute your flyers, so it's time to take advantage of all the options available. First, it's important to note the area you're planning on handing out flyers. Knowing your target market can make the leaflets more valuable.

Face To Face

Average Distribution of 150 Per/hr

It's tough to turn down a flyer from a friendly face on the street. Furthermore, if you train a small team of local hires to help sell the product to people on the streets, then they can turn just about anyone into a candle fanatic. With this highly engaged approach, you might find new customers faster than you think. Out of all the options, face-to-face might be the best available to you if you're looking for results. However, it can be disheartening as a lot of people will reject you, so don't be discouraged.

For increased legitimacy, you can provide your team with branded shirts to help show off your brand. This way, you're fully utilizing your distributors, making them an extension of your business down to the last stitch of embroidery.

Door To Door

Average Distribution of 70-100 Per/hr

Quick results where you choose volume over interaction is when you either send flyers to your customers or walk around neighborhoods placing them in random strangers' mailboxes. There are also a ton of companies that you can work with to do this for you. The only real downside is that you never really know if your flyers make it to the final destination. If they do, their conversion is low as promotional mail is usually tossed out relatively quickly.

Business To Business

Businesses have to stick together, and crafting great relationships with all the local establishments might prove beneficial. A business-to-business relationship can allow for your flyers to be displayed next to their tills, in their stores on bulletin boards, and you do the same in return. It's a no-brainer as you're both winning at the end of it all.

Pro Tip:

> Weather and timing are two significant factors in deciding to hand out flyers. You want to pick a time when there's a ton of foot traffic to have access to more people. Furthermore, you want to make sure the weather is optimal as nobody will waste their time talking to you in the rain, cold, wind, or excessive heat.

Tracking Conversion

Analyzing your flyer conversion rate is key as this helps you assess whether it is worth your marketing efforts. There are multiple ways in which you can track the success of your flyer's reach and value. First, understand that flyers are going to anyone and everyone. This means they aren't starting out as potential customers; you're hoping the flyer will change that. So how do you track success?

Unique URLs and QR Codes

One of the most effective means of realizing your flyers' effect is by including something unique only to the flyers. This can come in the form of a unique QR code or URLs, which allows you to track these specific avenues of traffic.

Special Offers or Discounts

Making a special or discount with a sense of urgency makes people act quicker to ensure they don't miss out. In addition, incentivizing readers of your flyer can boost sales and be an excellent ROI. Make sure that the discount code is specific to the flyer, that way you can actually track the success.

Increased Web Traffic, Social interaction, Phone Calls, and Emails

Before your flyers go out, take note of your daily averages in terms of traffic, social engagement/interaction, and how many inquiries you receive a day via email or social media.

Once the flyers go out, see if things change. For example, is your website getting more traffic as the flyers start going out? Or are you receiving more interaction on social media? Or are emails pouring in?

Key Takeaway

Don't be discouraged if you don't see results immediately. You can have varying success week-to-week, and nothing is guaranteed. Even a market where you kill it three weeks in a row can result in a terrible fourth week where you barely make anything. It's a gamble each time.

The benefits of doing a farmers market are far more convincing than any downfalls. First, you get to interact with your customers face-to-face and do market research out in the field with real people in real-time. Talk to them, ask them questions and find out what they like and don't like about your brand or product, and figure out if the complaints are common or if they're rare occurrences.

Another benefit is that you get to try things out in a soft-launch fashion to see how people respond to new products and see what works and what doesn't.

If you're going to utilize the farmers markets in your area, be sure to try and gain a following. Grow your social media and constantly post about your presence. Share pictures of your setup, the venue, highlight why people should attend, and attract more customers to come and see your stall.

There's no reason to ignore this opportunity and claim your stall to reach new customers organically and in person at the farmers market. Online retail is great, but sometimes nothing beats the connection of face-to-face shopping.

Chapter 9: Navigating Wholesale

Wholesale. It sounds scary, doesn't it? Well, you shouldn't be afraid of wholesale because your idea of wholesale probably is based on the misconceptions that it's massive orders worldwide. But guess what, that's wrong. Wholesale is just the art of selling your products through another person, business, or entity.

Think of it like this; you make your candles, then sell them to a retailer that sells them at a marked-up price in their store. It's not as cut and dry as the example, but that's the general idea behind wholesale on a more micro-scale.

In this chapter, we're going to break down everything you need to know about navigating the world of wholesale. By the time you've finished reading this, you'll be a master of the craft and ready to conquer the world.

Pricing Strategy

While every step in the wholesale process is vital to a thriving business, some carry more importance than others. The step that can kill your wholesale business in its tracks is an improper approach to pricing.

Underpricing your goods means you're losing money. Overpricing them isn't going to get you any sales. You need to find the sweet spot to price your products in a way that is fair to retailers while making you a profit.

There's a standard rule when it comes to pricing your candles for wholesale. The rule essentially states your products should be sold at a wholesale price which is 50% of the retail price. So if you usually sell your Summer Sunblast Candle for $10, the wholesale price you would offer is $5.

However, you need a profit margin of 50% or above to remain competitive and profitable. This is why you must sell your candles at a price that is 3/4x the cost of goods. This way, you'll make a profit, when you sell to wholesale customers as you can still give them that 50% discount and make money.

I know this may be confusing so let me explain with an example. You're selling a candle, it costs $7 to produce. You sell it on your own website at 3/4x cost, ie $28. You then want to sell the same candle to a wholesale customer. As they are buying a larger order and they too want to sell it at a profit, you will give them a discount (usually 50%) which makes it $14 per candle. This means even on wholesale orders you would still make $7 per candle profit.

Storefront

With one of the most important steps out of the way, it's time to set up an online storefront. A wholesale storefront isn't like your standard online store where anyone can just access it at any given time; this is a password-protected storefront for wholesale buyers.

You want legitimate businesses to have access to your wholesale storefront using a password, thus creating a barrier to entry. This is meant to help avoid non accredited companies, or individuals, from purchasing your products at wholesale prices.

There are numerous options for creating a password-protected online shop. My personal favorites would be Shopify's MagicPass or Faire. They're by no means the only available options, but they are amongst the best available. Shopify's MagicPass is perfect if you're on the Shopify+ plan. If your operation is on the larger side, then maybe consider using Faire.

Product Sourcing

You've got two options when it comes to candle production. Either you make everything yourself, or you work with a manufacturer to produce your custom designs. This is a very good option once you start selling wholesale as they can create products in much larger quantities, in less time, and the more you buy, usually the less it costs you per item.

You can discuss with manufacturers what your candle ought to look like and go back and forth with them until you get the design just right. Then, they'll produce prototypes for you to critique until you approve a final design and construction. However, this will take months and can cost you quite a bit for each prototype you receive. Additionally, there are various other fees attached to the process which you need to be wary of. I will not go into details in this book as this is a whole other subject on its own, but make sure you do your due diligence and research before beginning with this process.

Things to Consider When Sourcing Products

1.Shipping Cost

Discuss with your chosen manufacturer or top options to determine their shipping costs to evaluate your best option. Then, ensure you take note or inquire about free shipping offers for oversized orders.

2. Minimum Order Quantity (MOQ)

You need to have a clear understanding of the minimum order quantity requirement of your manufacturing options. For example, while one can offer outstanding shipping fees, they might require you to order a quantity far too oversized for your needs.

3. Turnaround Time

From the get-go, you need to know how long the initial order will take and how long replenishing stock will take in the future. You need to know your turnaround times in order to manage your inventory, to ensure you have enough products in stock, especially when you have an unexpected order!

4. Manufacturing Times

How long does it take to make your products? You want the most efficient manufacturing partner who's good at what they do both in terms of quality and speed. The more knowledge you have about the ins and outs of your manufacturer, the more you're able to plan ahead.

5. Always Look for the Asterix* (Hidden Fees)

This is arguably the most important point. You need to talk straight with your chosen manufacturer about what all their fees are, from placing the order to receiving the order. You don't want to be caught off guard by some crazy figures at the end of your order, not realizing they charged for X and Y.

Pro Tip:

> Always ensure that your lawyer looks over the contract before you sign it to make sure you understand any loopholes, hidden fees or potential issues that could arise.

Policies and contractual agreements

You need to be the master of your ship when it comes to your wholesale business, and that means setting policies for both you and your customers to follow, from purchasing and payments to timelines.

Set the MOQ

Setting minimum order quantities (MOQ) requires retailers to buy a minimum amount of products to be eligible for purchase. It's important to note that the less time-consuming it is to produce a certain product, the lower the MOQ should be.

Set the sample policy

I recommend offering free samples for products that are easy to produce and don't take much time. This can really seal the deal for some retailers as they can see firsthand what they're spending their money on. However, if the wholesale customer wants a large sample pack which is labor-intensive to produce, you are better off charging the customer. You don't want to wind up making hundreds of sample orders for free, losing you time and money. Whether you're providing free samples or samples at a cost, I recommend always charging for shipping. However, this decision is up to you and your business, this is just advice and it may not apply to everyone.

Consider Bulk Discounts

You want to incentivize retailers to buy as much as possible from your business. An excellent method of inflating orders is offering discounts for bulk purchases. The higher the quantity, the bigger the discount. For example, if a retailer orders 100 candles, they're sold at $12 each. However, if they order 500 candles, then you offer it to them at $10 each.

Pro Tip:

> Remember what we said earlier, never go below double your cost per item, you need to make profit and ensure it is worth your time and effort.

Minimum Order Price

Setting a minimum order price means you're setting an amount required to even place an initial order. This isn't in terms of quantity but a dollar value. This can create a barrier to entry that forces you to lose out on some businesses. However, if you've got a certain amount of costs to meet to make the order worth it, this can ensure you don't lose out on money.

Define and Write Payment Terms

Protect yourself and your wholesale business against losses by setting payment terms for retail customers to adhere to when purchasing.

Extended or Net Terms

This gives retailers a hard deadline for payments of goods. The most common extended terms are Net 30/60/90 and are always expressed as Net + the number of days. You have the choice of making the Extended or Net Terms begin when the order is either shipped out or received. To make this extra clear, here is an example. Let's say you chose Net 30 to begin when the order is shipped. This means 30 days after shipment, the wholesale customer needs to pay their invoice.

Extended Terms With Prompt Payment Discount

Prompt Payment Discount is when you offer discounts for payments received a certain amount of time before the extended terms expire. This method helps to improve cash flow which is often crucial in SME's (small to medium enterprises). Therefore, this is a useful method to know about and use.

The Prompt Payment Discount policy is represented as X/A Net D.

X = Discount

A = Days to Qualify

Net D = Extend Terms

For example, 10/20 Net 30 means you'll give a 10% discount if the retailer pays within 20 days under the 30 days extended terms.

Proforma

Proforma is when you ship your products out immediately after receiving payment from the retailer.

Advanced Deposit

An advanced deposit is when a customer pays some of the overall amount of their purchase when ordering the product and the rest upon receiving the product.

Sale or Return (SOR)

A SOR is when you allow retailers to return what they don't sell, meaning you're only making money on the units they do sell. This is a less common option but one that can be good when working with smaller retailers. For example, if you are working with a local store, they may not have an idea of the quantity they may sell yet, so this could be a great option for them to test out your products at the start of your relationship.

Determine Shipping Costs

There are two ways to approach shipping. The first way is by making it the responsibility of the retailers to pay for the shipment of their orders. You should allow them to choose from various shipping vendors in case they have a preference. However, because candles are fragile, you may need to pre-select only reliable shippers that you can trust with fragile goods.

Suppose you plan to take on the delivery fees and offer free or discounted shipping to your customers. In this case, you should look at trying to create a deal with some reliable and affordable shipping companies. A contract with a trusted shipping company can save you time, money, and headaches.

Pro Tip:

> When choosing a shipping provider, ensure they can adhere to a pickup schedule that works with your production quantities and timelines.

If you're looking to broker a Freight contract, then maybe try FreightPros. They provide quotes from vetted and highly qualified freight carriers with discounts.

Payment Collection Options

You need to determine the best way possible to collect payments from retailers. You can do this through an invoicing system like FreshBooks, QuickBooks, and Invoicera. These are all systems which send automatic invoices to your wholesale customers. An invoice can send them to your buyer's tab, where they can process their payment when it's due. You can use a variety of payment solutions like Stripe, Paypal, Payment Cloud, Square Payments, and Quickbook Payments.

Alternatively, you can use Afterpay or other delayed payment apps to send invoices and automatically charge buyers on the specified payment dates.

Product Photography

This is something you should already be prepared for (see Chapter 2), considering you've done this for your website and social media, right? The rules are no different; retailers want what individual customers want, transparency and clarity regarding your product. Therefore, you need to provide all the information possible to retailers as well as clear photos so they know what they're purchasing.

If you think a customer won't take a chance on your product with poor product photography, best believe another business won't even consider giving you a second glance.

Line Sheet/Inventory Catalogue

A line sheet or inventory catalog is where retailers will go to view and order your products. A line sheet or inventory catalog includes;

- Product Images
- Product Description
- Product ID Numbers
- Product Names
- Other Vital Information

Make sure your line sheets are easy to read, well-formatted, and organized while providing all the necessary information about your products. Be sure to include branding within the line sheet but make it subtle as the focus should be on the products.

To create a line sheet, you can either;

1. Use Photoshop and do it yourself,

2. Hire a professional either locally or on Fiverr,
3. Use a platform like NuOrder to create and update line sheets for you.

Look For Buyers

You are now closer than ever to tapping into the world of wholesale. All you need now is customers. There are numerous ways to approach potential buyers for your candles and we're going to explore each available option. Of course, boutiques, gift stores and home goods stores will be a bulk of your target market, but there are always other options to consider. Maybe write a list of retailers you want to work with and create goals as a guideline to grow your wholesale business before going out and conquering a larger scene.

Here are some of the ways you can find and win over buyers for your wholesale candle business.

Website

Soley this isn't something I'd recommend if you're just starting out or if your brand isn't fairly known. However, if you feel like you want to attempt to win over some customers through your website, then you're more than welcome to try! Provide a link on your website to access the wholesale website you set up or a place to inquire. Then run ads through Google and utilize SEO to promote this part of your business to retailers.

Complementary

Make some calls, send some emails, take to the streets! Pitch your product high and low to complementary businesses. Spread the word about your business and if your pitch is good enough, you could have some potential orders!

If you're going to pitch your product in writing, then keep your verbiage below ten sentences. Focus on why your business and product would be a good fit for them. Furthermore, include a line sheet to showcase your product with relevant information.

If you're going in person, be sure to take some business cards, maybe some hard copies of your line sheet, and even a sample or two if you want to go the extra mile. Of course, a free product won't guarantee a sale down the line, but it could improve your chances.

Once you've approached the business the first time, make sure to keep following up. Remember, the sales pitch only ends when they say yes, or provide a definitive no.

Trade Shows

Trade shows are a great way to connect with retailers in a setting designed to do just that, connect business to business (B2B). Take a look at a Wholesale Directory like Wholesale Central and find a trade show which may fit your business. Be on the lookout for some complementary businesses when picking out trade shows, for example, soap or room spray companies. Finally, prepare to attend the trade show and set up a make-shift storefront in a provided space. This is an essential part of promoting your product and brand, so be sure you're ready (see chapter 8 to learn everything you need to know about how to set up a stall).

Online Wholesale Marketplaces

If you're looking to get your business out there, then wholesale marketplaces are perfect for your products. Retailers often turn to wholesale marketplaces due to the convenience of shopping for everything in one place. It's kind of like a virtual trade show if you think about it!

Look around for some of the best wholesale marketplace options and determine which one works best for you. Some of the options include; Alibaba, Joor, Faire, Tundra, and Handshake. Also, note that you can exist on multiple marketplaces as long as you're up for the admin!

Community Groups

Another avenue to try when it comes to retail outreach is joining community groups like the Boutique Hub, which connects you to boutiques of varying sizes using a genuine community-based approach.

Pros and Cons of Wholesale

Here are some of the pros and cons you'll encounter when deciding to break into the world of wholesale.

Pros

1.Volume

You're going to be selling your product in excess, well that's the plan at least! But, as you start developing good relationships with your retailers, you'll see your overall revenue grow both quicker and more consistently.

You want to focus on building these relationships and getting repeat business from them, as this can provide a somewhat predictable income.

2. Marketing is out of your hands

If you're not a fan of marketing, but you're a fan of making money doing what you love, then let me tell you you're going to love wholesale. Beyond initial marketing to the retailer, once you've secured the deal, it's pretty much over. You're not selling to their customers; that's their job! You need to convince a business to sell your product which is far easier than convincing the equivalent number of customers to purchase a candle. Another benefit is that you're still gaining brand awareness through their marketing of your product which makes this aspect of wholesale all the more beneficial.

3. Control Sales With MOQ

You have the power to set a MOQ. Setting the right MOQ for your business means you're giving yourself more room to make accurate forecasts of sales and revenues. But, adversely, MOQs might scare off new customers. Hence, you need to really consider your options, especially at the beginning of your wholesale journey.

4. Easy to Convince

The more retailers you have under your belt, the easier it becomes to convince new retailers to sell your product. You've got credibility in numbers, especially if you're selling to quality retailers. You should always be striving to build a wholesale empire. Hunting for bigger and better retailers to expand your operations and, more importantly, your revenue and profit margins.

5. Fixed Profit Margins

Your concerns over profits aren't as relative when it comes to wholesale as opposed to selling through your own website or store. Your focus needs to be more on quantity. The more you sell, the more you make; therefore, the more profit you generate. Volume is the real driver of increasing your overall success in both earnings and profit. Considering that your profit margin is fixed, your focus should be on making the orders as big as possible. When equated to what you'd need to sell yourself to achieve the exact same numbers, bulk order earnings will show the great divide between these two avenues.

Cons

1.Capital

Going wholesale isn't going to come cheap. While the financial gain of starting a wholesale business is evident, the initial cost of setting up a wholesale business comes at a hefty price.

Considering you need to buy your initial stock in volume, work with delivery methods to get products to retail, all while maintaining sufficient stock, you'll find that the initial capital investment isn't cheap. However, don't let this scare you off! Wholesale is a rewarding avenue to take for your business, even if it takes a bit of time to reap those profits.

2. Large Quantities or No Sale

This works both on a manufacturer and wholesale customer level. Suppose you don't want to order in bulk or are simply unable to do so. This could cause a rocky or non-existent relationship with manufacturers. Additionally, if you don't have your products in stock for retailers, they may be less inclined to purchase from you. You need to be able to provide quantity and quality always. This means costly bulk ordering from your chosen manufacturer.

3. Large Overhead

You need to be prepared to fulfill orders for retailers at a moment's notice, which means you need to have the stock ready to go! As a result, you're going to constantly be holding onto a lot of stock at any given time. Unfortunately, this means you have a ton of cash tied to that inventory.

4. Increased Demand For Space

You're going to be selling to a lot of retailers, hopefully. This means you're going to be making and packaging a ton of candles. You're going to have to store all these candles somewhere, which means you need adequate space for your finished products. Don't venture too deep into wholesale without having this nailed down, even if it's just options available to acquire when necessary. You don't want to have to become a case study for hoarders where you've got boxes upon boxes of candles all over your home, office, workshop, garage, and anywhere else they can be placed that isn't a single dedicated location.

5. Lower Profit Margins

You're discounting your products, and in doing so, your profit margins won't be the same as they might be with retail. Profit margins for retail usually range from 10-20%, while wholesale is 2-8%. However, you're in the candle business, and this is where research can really come in handy to try and optimize your prices to the point where maybe, just maybe, you find a sweet spot that actually defies the norms and makes you a little bit extra. I wouldn't be disappointed with these lower profit margins overall. Focus on optimizing your overall costs to bring them down to their cheapest point, get your money's worth on every aspect of your candle production, storage, and distribution, and work towards increasing your margins wherever possible.

6. Possibility of Losses

Anything you do comes with risks, and the possibility of loss is one that you can experience greatly with wholesale. This is primarily due to the fact that you've got to hold a lot of stock, this is essentially tied up money. Additionally, there are some added risks, make sure you're storing your products correctly to decrease the risk of any potential damage and always take out insurance. When choosing a room to store your finished products, make sure the risk of water damage, fire, and insects/vermin is low.

Pro Tip:

> Anything you can't sell to retailers for whatever possible reason doesn't have to be considered a lost cause. While you can return it to a manufacturer in some very rare cases, that's not your only option. Instead, get creative and try revitalizing the products and selling them locally for less than you'd typically charge. Yes, it will take longer to get rid of the excess stock, but you won't have lost money on idle products clogging up your storage!

Key Takeaway

While there is so much to consider when venturing into wholesale, you can't ignore the immense possibilities of this avenue. There are so many ways to make wholesale a lucrative part of your business. Starting is the most challenging part. It gets easier as you start fine-tuning your wholesale practices and nailing down all the finer details such as distribution, production, operations, and logistics. Once these things have been narrowed down or achieved, then the sky's the limit!

As you progress through this process, never take any one step for granted, wholesale relies on a unified approach that's well thought out, implemented, and maintained throughout. If done right, you'll never look back. You'll be too busy producing candles like the world is about to lose electricity forever!

Conclusion

I don't know about you, but I'm exhausted. The good news is we both made it here together! This was an intensive journey but so rewarding. When I learned these things the first time, I remember being so overwhelmed just at the sheer volume of information. The great news is you own this book. So, you've got it as a reference to go back to any time you need. That's what I'd hoped for! To impart my knowledge so far to you while leaving behind a reference with all the answers.

After nine intensive chapters, I hope you feel more excited about all the possibilities that exist to grow your business, make more connections, and achieve more sales. Social media is one of the most challenging things a business has to contend with. Still, the rewards are so beneficial that it's hard to ignore them.

We did it all! We looked at why your business isn't succeeding right now and how to fix it. We explored ways to get online, get on social media, interact with influencers, email, PR, in-person selling and even wholesale! You've got a more robust foundation now than you had before. Now, it's time to focus on building your successful business! It's time for you to take the lessons you have learnt from this book and seize these opportunities that are at your fingertips.

You've got the tools, you've got the knowledge, now it is time to go out and put it all to the test! Good luck. I know you're going to crush it and sell tons of candles online, in-store, at farmers markets and as a wholesaler. I can't wait to see you succeed!

REVIEW

If you enjoyed reading this book, please leave a review on Amazon. It's through reviews and ongoing support that I can keep providing content like this.

Additionally, if you would like to join a Facebook group full of incredibly supportive candle makers then join the Candle Making Business 101 group using the link below:
www.facebook.com/group/candlemakingbusiness101

A FREE GIFT TO OUR READERS!

A free copy of **11 Easy Tricks to Master your Candle Launch and Triple your Sales within the First Month!**

Visit this link to get your copy now:
www.graceholmesbook.com

References

39 Top Benefits of Email Marketing for Small Business (with Examples). (2021, September 27). Constant Contact. https://blogs.constantcontact.com/benefits-of-email-marketing/

5 Great Marketing Quotes that Will Radically Change Your Client Attraction Success. Global Institute for Travel Entrepreneurs. https://www.travelbusinessu.com/5-great-marketing-quotes-that-will-radically-change-your-client-attraction-success-2/

Auxier, B., & Anderson, M. (2021, April 7). *Social Media Use in 2021*. Pew Research Center: Internet, Science & Tech. https://www.pewresearch.org/internet/2021/04/07/social-media-use-in-2021/Bhatoa, S. (2021, May 11). *The importance of quality photography for your eCommerce*. Splento Blog: Videography & Photography on Demand.

https://www.splento.com/blog/photography/the-importance-of-quality-photography-for-your-ecommerce/

Bonner, M. (2014, June 24). *From a PR Expert: How to Get Magazines to Feature Your Products*. CreativeLive Blog. https://www.creativelive.com/blog/how-to-get-featured-in-magazines/

Bruiet, F. (2019, April 30). *How product photography impact e-commerce performance*. Meero. https://www.meero.com/en/news/e_commerce/511/1900-how-great-product-photographs-influence-e-commerce-websites-conversions-en

Dragilev, D. (2021, September 16). *PR Outreach: How To Do It Right in 2021 w/ Templates, Examples & Tips*. JustReachOut Blog. https://blog.justreachout.io/pr-outreach/Geyser, W. (2021, September 28). TikTok

Etsy Shop On Pinterest!- 2021. CedCommerce Blog. https://cedcommerce.com/blog/promote-etsy-on-pinterest/

Email Marketing Is a Double Win for Customer Acquisition, Retention. (2016, July 21). EMarketer. https://www.emarketer.com/Article/Email-Marketing-Double-Win-Customer-Acquisition-Retention/1014239 F. (n.d.). *Coding, UX and Digital Content - Digital Marketing Course - FutureLearm*. FutureLearn. https://www.futurelearn.com/experttracks/coding-app-marketing

Geyser, W. (2021a, August 18). *The State of Influencer Marketing 2021: Benchmark Report*. Influencer Marketing Hub. https://influencermarketinghub.com/influencer-marketing-benchmark-report-2021/The Grin.co. (2021, August 25). *How to Write an Effective Influencer Collaboration Email*. GRIN - Influencer Marketing Software. https://grin.co/blog/how-to-write-an-effective-influencer-collaboration-email/

Handbook. (2021, June 23). *How To Contact Influencers And Get A Positive Response*. https://www.thehandbook.com/celebrity-news/tips-for-contacting-influencers-2/

Ho, L. (2021, March 3). *How to Contact Instagram Influencers: The Perfect Process for 2021*. Inzpire.Me Blog. https://blog.inzpire.me/how-to-contact-instagram-influencers/

Jain, A. S. (2021, September 22). *Top 10 Benefits and Disadvantages of Online Shopping*. ToughNickel. https://toughnickel.com/frugal-living/Online-shopping-sites-benefits

Journal, W. S. (n.d.). *ETSY | Etsy Inc. Annual Income Statement - WSJ*. Wall Street Journal. https://www.wsj.com/market-data/quotes/ETSY/financials/annual/income-statement

Kirsch, K. (2021, August 14). *The Ultimate List of Email Marketing Stats for 2021*. Hubspot. https://blog.hubspot.com/marketing/email-marketing-stats?__hstc=118989590.453d9afcce699c1ae7c19e38f3dfc c52.1632202542882.1632202542882.1632202542882.1& hssc=118989590.1.1632202542883& hsfp=1310990955 Hill, M. (2016, May 31).

L. (2021, September 22). *Influencer Marketing ROI: How to measure your campaigns*. Storyclash. https://www.storyclash.com/blog/en/influencer-marketing-roi/

MacDonald, S. (2021, May 10). *Email Open Rates: A Scientific, Step by Step Guide for 2021*. Super Office. https://www.superoffice.com/blog/email-open-rates/

MarketingSherpa (2016, January 7). *Email Research Chart: How often customers want to receive promotional emails*. MarketingSherpa. https://www.marketingsherpa.com/article/chart/how-customers-want-promo-emails

Mediakix. (2020, October 9). Influencer Tiers for the Influencer Marketing Industry. https://mediakix.com/influencer-marketing-resources/influencer-tiers/

Nesbitt, M. (2020, August 10). Why Product Photography is Important to Your Business. Medium. https://medium.com/@morgannesbitt/why-product-photography-is-important-to-your-business-941eb64dc6b2

NinjaOutreach. (2016, March 30). *Antonio*. https://ninjaoutreach.com/email-marketing-tips/

Patel, N. (2021, September 2). *How to Increase Your Website Traffic Without SEO*. Neil Patel.

https://neilpatel.com/blog/how-to-increase-website-traffic-without-seo/

Pengue, M. (2021, June 30). Etsy Statistics: Buyers Demographics, Revenues, and Sales. WBL. https://writersblocklive.com/blog/etsy-statistics/

Simon @ DMI. (2021, October 27). *20 Surprising Influencer Marketing Statistics*. Digital Marketing Institute. .

Revenue, Users & Engagement Stats (2021). Influencer Marketing Hub. Retrieved November 6, 2021, from https://influencermarketinghub.com/tiktok-stats/

Sehl, K. (2019, January 24). *Pinterest Ads: A Simple Guide to Set You Up For Success*. Social Media Marketing & Management Dashboard. https://blog.hootsuite.com/pinterest-ads/

Santora, J. (2019, December 19). *Email Marketing vs. Social Media: Is There a Clear Winner?* OptinMonster. https://optinmonster.com/email-marketing-vs-social-media-performance-2016-2019-statistics/

Statista. (2021, November 11). *Pinterest: number of monthly active users worldwide 2016–2021*. https://www.statista.com/statistics/463353/pinterest-global-mau/

Tasneem, S. (2021, September 13). *Everything You Need To Know About Promoting Your* Trösch, D. (2020, July 20). *How to Email Influencers to Promote Your Product (5 of the Best Ways)*. Fourstarzz Media.

https://www.fourstarzz.com/post/how-to-email-influencers-to-promote-your-product

Vistaprint Ideas & Advice. (n.d.). *The Ultimate Guide to Creating Flyers & Leaflets | Vistaprint UK*. Vistaprint Blog UK. https://www.vistaprint.co.uk/hub/guide-creating-flyers

West, C. (2021, March 3). *23 Pinterest stats and facts marketers must know in 2021*. Sprout Social. https://sproutsocial.com/insights/pinterest-statistics/

Wholesaling: A Whole Bunch of Pros and Cons – Ordoro Blog. (2016, March 30). Ordoro. https://blog.ordoro.com/2016/03/30/wholesaling-a-whole-bunch-of-pros-and-cons/

Printed in Great Britain
by Amazon

22359549R00142